PING-PONG

PING-PONG

By Arthur Adamov

A Play in Two Parts

Translated by Richard Howard

GROVE PRESS, INC.   **NEW YORK**

Library of Congress Catalog Card Number: 59-7436

Originally published as LE PING-PONG in
Théâtre II, Librairie Gallimard, Paris, 1955

The translator would like to express his thanks to Mr. Robert Cordier, director of the first New York production of *Ping-Pong*, for his constant collaboration in preparing this version.

Ping-Pong is published in three editions:

An Evergreen Book (E-154)

A cloth bound edition

A specially bound and signed edition
of 26 copies lettered A through Z
and 4 copies, *hors commerce*, numbered 1 through 4

*Grove Press Books and Evergreen Books
are published by Barney Rosset at Grove Press, Inc.*
795 Broadway   New York 3, N. Y.

Distributed in Canada by McClelland & Stewart Ltd.,
25 Hollinger Road, Toronto 16

Type set by The Polyglot Press, New York

MANUFACTURED IN THE UNITED STATES OF AMERICA

Characters:

ARTHUR
VICTOR
MRS. DURANTY
SUTTER
MR. ROGER
ANNETTE
THE OLD MAN

PING-PONG *was first produced on March 2, 1955 in Paris under the direction of Jacques Mauclair.*

PART ONE

SCENE ONE

(*The Gayety Cafe. Stage right a table and some chairs; stage left the bar. In the rear, not far from the bar, a pinball machine.*

Arthur, a nervous, carelessly dressed young man in a pullover, is playing the pinball machine. His friend, Victor, a tall, gangling young man wearing a sweatshirt, is watching him play.

Sitting behind the bar in a black shawl and ruffles, Mrs. Duranty, about 60, wizened and whining, is reading The Figaro.)

ARTHUR:
   (*Playing the pinball machine*)
   What's got into her today? There's something wrong. See? It came down full speed!

VICTOR:
   I don't want to butt in, but considering the way you sent it up . . .

ARTHUR:

I sent it up the way I always do and that doesn't . . .

VICTOR:

Now you're not going to start again.

ARTHUR:

(*Who has sent up another ball*)
All right. Here we go! The four top numbers, all at the
same time. Look!

VICTOR:

First of all, watch what you're doing. Your flipper! No,
the left one!

ARTHUR:

It doesn't work. How can I help it? Mrs. Duranty, your
left flipper doesn't work.

MRS. DURANTY:

Of course it doesn't. You play like wild men. If you press
both buttons at once, of course you jam them. I've told
you that a hundred times already. If you keep on like this,
you're going to kill her for me.

VICTOR:

Please, Mrs. Duranty. Arthur doesn't know how to play,
there's no doubt about that. But still that doesn't mean
your machine works any better. There she is and here we
are!

MRS. DURANTY:

You, you have a reason for everything!

VICTOR:

(To Arthur)

Allow me.

(He takes Arthur's place and sends up a new ball; then, triumphantly)

I regret to inform you, my dear Arthur, but the left flipper . . .

(He stamps his foot)

Now that's really too much!

ARTHUR:

What was I saying? She balks every other time.

(He pushes Victor away.)

VICTOR:

It's not your turn! . . . I cut my class again today, and all I do is watch you . . . play.

ARTHUR:

Victor, we agreed to take turns. If you didn't want to you should have said so sooner.

(He plays and loses)

VICTOR:

(Laughing)

Foiled again!

(Enter stage right Sutter, about 40, tall, strong, a man who takes up room, a lot of room, waves his arms, walks about, and scratches himself while he talks. He is wearing a light suit of dubious elegance and carrying a briefcase.)

SUTTER:

Good morning, Mrs. Duranty.

MRS. DURANTY:
(Putting down her newspaper)
Good morning, Mr. Sutter.

SUTTER:
(Leaning on the bar)
And how are we this morning?

MRS. DURANTY:
Well, the kidneys are a little better, but now the legs have
it. . . .
(Whining)
It twinges and twitches so—it doesn't stop for a moment.
It's merciless.
(Pause)
What will you have, Mr. Sutter?

SUTTER:
A cinzano. Faithful to cinzano!
(Looking around him)
The Gayety's rather quiet today.

MRS. DURANTY:
(Pouring out Sutter's drink)
You don't have to tell me!

SUTTER:
(Shrugging his shoulders, throwing up his hands)
Ah, the mysteries of commerce!
(Heading toward Victor and Arthur)
Excuse me for interrupting your revels, my young friends,
but
(Pointing to the pinball machine)

I have to open up this demon's belly. Business before pleasure!

(*He pushes Arthur and Victor out of the way*)

VICTOR:

(*Wanting to make a good impression while Sutter is preparing to open the machine*)

Well what do you know! I always thought our money went somewhere, but I've never watched the operation before.

SUTTER:

Yes, that's how it is. You sow and I reap.

(*He removes a tremendous pile of coins from the machine*)

Oh, she's been eating pretty well.

MRS. DURANTY:

It's easy to see you weren't collecting when Charles was alive.

(*She crosses herself*)

SUTTER:

(*Putting the money on the bar*)

Poor man!

(*Pause*)

Cancer is the scourge of modern life.

MRS. DURANTY:

(*Counting the money*)

When he put the pinball machine in, business improved a little.

SUTTER:

Of course it did. Natural curiosity—the attraction of novelty!

(*He shows his empty glass which Mrs. Duranty fills again*)

ARTHUR:

(*Still standing next to the pinball machine, nudging Victor who is as fascinated as he is by Sutter*)

I thought we came here to play.

VICTOR:

So go ahead. What're you waiting for?

MRS. DURANTY:

(*Looking up*)

Only now they're everywhere! I've even heard they're going to open "pinball parlors," whole rooms

(*Pointing despairingly*)

with nothing but them!

SUTTER:

Oh, that's just a crackpot scheme: there's many a slip . . .

MRS. DURANTY:

They only come in here now so they can break this one for me!

VICTOR:

(*Taking the opportunity to enter the conversation while Arthur is playing furiously*)

I hope you're not referring to us, Mrs. Duranty.

MRS. DURANTY:

As if you were the only ones in the world.

(*To Sutter*)

And the repairs. It's so complicated. As soon as you need a workman, he's always sick. So between the sick ones and the clumsy ones . . .

(*Sutter laughs, leaning against the bar. Enter stage right Mr. Roger, a refined young man in a threadbare jacket with a flower in his buttonhole.*)

MRS. DURANTY:

(*Pouncing on him*)

No, no, not you, Mr. Roger. I won't serve you. Just so you can make fun of my machine, no thank you!

MR. ROGER:

It's not a question of *your* machine. I just don't happen to like that sort of amusement, that's all, and I don't see why I shouldn't say so. Believe me, Mrs. Duranty, you're wrong to play the dictators' game. It's not one of your attributes.

MRS. DURANTY:

My what?

MR. ROGER:

I was afraid you wouldn't understand. Forget it. And since I've always paid for my drinks, I'll thank you to serve me now.

MRS. DURANTY:

No. Go somewhere else and drink.

(*Arthur starts to intervene in behalf of Mr. Roger, but Victor plucks his sleeve to hold him back.*)

Besides young ladies don't like cafes without pinball machines.

SUTTER:

Young ladies play it smart.

MRS. DURANTY:

And anyway she hasn't come today, and even if she had I wouldn't tell you.

(*Sighing*)

Poor little thing.

MR. ROGER:

Really, Mrs. Duranty, you're fantastic. Is it my fault if those ridiculous machines are both stupid and vulgar?

SUTTER:

Young man, you don't know what ears your words are falling on.

MR. ROGER:

No, I don't, but even if you were the president of this business I'd say the same thing.

SUTTER:

Have you ever really thought about this game that seems so contemptible to you? No? Silence then, back to work! (*He takes his share of the money from the bar and puts it in his briefcase.*)

MRS. DURANTY:

(*Shaking her apron*)

All right now, out!

MR. ROGER:

All right. I know when I'm not wanted.

(*Contemptuously indicating Arthur and Victor*)
Besides, I can see you prefer a really select clientele.
(*He exits.*)

MRS. DURANTY:

(*Returning behind the bar*)
He hasn't a penny, he hasn't a job, and he always acts proud as a peacock. To think some girl could be interested in a prig like that!
(*She picks up her newspaper again.*)

SUTTER:

Signs of the times.

VICTOR:

It's funny, I don't know that fellow from Adam, but I must admit he made a bad impression on me from the first moment I saw him. That flower-in-your-buttonhole type when his feet are coming through his shoes . . .

ARTHUR:

I don't see why he shouldn't have the right . . .

SUTTER:

(*Laughing*)
Chivalry is not dead!

MRS. DURANTY:

(*Looking up from her newspaper*)
Another raid in Algeria. Those people! The minute they can cut someone's throat . . .

VICTOR:

Watch out, Mrs. Duranty. You're talking just like the fascists.

SUTTER:

And I suppose the Algerians aren't fascists?

ARTHUR:

Why should they be?

MRS. DURANTY:

And what about the Germans?

VICTOR:

(*Shrugging his shoulders*)
What's the connection?

MRS. DURANTY:

They're all *voyeurs*.

SUTTER:

(*Laughing*)
Explain that one to us, Mrs. Duranty.

MRS. DURANTY:

I mean what I say: I've never seen an Algerian play the machine. Not once. They come in and they watch. It doesn't cost anything: why bother? And the Germans do the same thing.

SUTTER:

The Germans are calculators. They may hold back sometimes, but that's so they can observe, estimate the risks. The only thing that surprises me is that the machines in Germany aren't as popular as they should be normally. I was in Heidelberg last month on business. Charming, Heidelberg. And as for pretty girls . . .

(*Arthur and Victor have begun playing again, but they can't keep from watching Sutter at almost every moment.*

*He seems, according to their gestures, to stupefy Victor and
exasperate Arthur. Enter Annette, a tall, thin, pretty girl
with a discontented expression; she wears her hair long.
Victor nudges Arthur to indicate that Annette has come in.
A perpetual exchange of signals begins between them: curi-
ousity and admiration regarding Annette, bewilderment and
rage regarding Sutter.)*

MRS. DURANTY:

Why it's Annette!

ANNETTE:

Yes. I was in the neighborhood and I thought I'd drop in
to say hello.

MRS. DURANTY:

(Kissing Annette)
My little sweetheart, thinking of me!

SUTTER:

(To Arthur and Victor, to attract Annette's attention)
Take it easy, boys, easy. Don't play with your nerves:
control yourselves.
(To Annette, who has burst out laughing)
Don't laugh, Miss. Self-mastery is the greatest conquest
of all.

ANNETTE:

Do you consider the machine a conquest too?

SUTTER:

Yes, and you a princess: Mrs. Duranty doesn't consider
me worthy of being introduced to a princess.

Mrs. Duranty:

Oh dear, I'm forgetting everything. My poor head!
(*Making the introductions*)
This is Annette. Her mother was an old friend of mine.
And this is Mr. Sutter. He comes here often
(*Lowering her voice*)
for the machine!

(*Sutter and Annette shake hands. Sutter puts his arm around Annette's shoulders and sweeps her off toward a table. Annette frees herself*)

Annette:

By the way, Mrs. Duranty, if you still haven't seen "Ben Franklin's First Affair" you should. It's really *your* kind of movie.

Mrs. Duranty:

But it's so far away, dear. With these poor legs—
(*She hobbles back behind the bar*)

Sutter:

(*Sitting down beside Annette*)
You're a strange girl, Annette. . . . Judging from appearances I would never have guessed you were such a fervent enthusiast of the silver screen. It's such a passive kind of entertainment. . . . "Passive pleasure is no pleasure" . . .
(*Pointing to the pinball machine*)
Now if you're talking about real amusement, here's my choice, right over here. Action! Conflict! Participation!
(*Pause*)

But I'm wasting time preaching to a convert. I'm sure you
love the little monster as much as I do.

ANNETTE:

Well, platonically, I suppose. It's always so popular: not
just anyone can get at it.

(*She indicates Arthur and Victor*)

SUTTER:

Your wish is my command. I'll deliver it into your hands
on the spot.

(*He approaches Arthur and Victor*)

Gentlemen, this young lady would like a turn at the
machine.

ARTHUR:

(*To Sutter*)

I would have invited her myself but I didn't want to seem
indiscreet.

(*To Annette*)

The machine is yours, Miss.

(*Arthur and Victor step aside*)

ANNETTE:

(*Standing up*)

Really? You're sure you don't mind?

VICTOR:

Not at all. On condition

(*Laughing*)

that you're equal to the occasion.

MRS. DURANTY:

You'd be foolish not to try it, dear. . . .

ANNETTE:

(*Beginning to play*)

I don't understand a thing. All those numbers lighting up
. . . and it doesn't even reach a million.

ARTHUR:

I see that you don't know her . . . otherwise you'd have
already wondered—the way I have—if it's only a matter
of chance . . .

VICTOR:

(*Annoyed by Arthur and determined to make Annette
notice him*)

There are machines and machines. For instance, the one
at the Palm Tree where I usually . . .

MRS. DURANTY:

(*Shrilly*)

Well, why don't you go back to the Palm Tree if it's such
a habit!

SUTTER:

(*Who has been waiting for a chance to speak*)

Chance, habit—words, words, words.

(*To Annette*)

First light up the top row of numbers. You see? Both sides.
That's the hardest. When those light up . . . But you're not
aiming. You have to aim. Always aim. A hunter's eye . . .

(*Pause*)

May I?

ARTHUR:
 (*To Sutter*)
 Why don't you wait until Miss . . .

ANNETTE:
 (*Laughing*)
 No, let him go ahead. Look at him. He's like a force of nature.

SUTTER:
 Go on, laugh, all of you. Let the future be my judge.
 (*He plays and wins*)
 The top flippers, it's all in the top flippers. One ball, five free games. You're astounded, aren't you?

ANNETTE:
 Rather.

(*Arthur and Victor, irritated, signal to each other*)

SUTTER:
 Nevertheless, it's not so surprising as you might think.
 (*Pause*)
 I suppose you've never asked yourself where a machine like this comes from, what kind of head conceives such inventions? Well, I'll tell you because I happen to know that head, I'd recognize it in a thousand. When I was a little boy that head shared a desk with me. In other words, the president of the Corporation is no less than Sutter's childhood friend!

MRS. DURANTY:
 (*Emerging from her mental no man's land*)
 You know, I always suspected something like that.

ARTHUR:

(*To Sutter, while Victor plucks at his sleeve*)

Excuse me, but if that's the case, why are you only collecting . . .

SUTTER:

(*With a particularly eloquent gesture*)

Only collecting! I didn't collect yesterday and I won't be collecting tomorrow. Wherever there are wheels turning, Sutter's at the axle! Administrator, prospector . . .

ANNETTE:

(*Amused*)

Prospector? That sounds good! What does a prospector do?

SUTTER:

He takes the public's temperature. He's here, he's there, he's everywhere—no one's too big, no one's too small for him. He keeps his eyes open, his nose to the grindstone, his ear to the ground. His mission? To keep the Corporation informed as to how the players feel—their tastes, their wishes, the changes they expect, the reforms they hope for.

(*Pause*)

It's a hard task but it's well-paid. As a matter of fact, would you be interested in that kind of work, yourself?

ANNETTE:

You know, I'm only an usherette and I never . . .

MRS. DURANTY:

Yes, Annette's an usherette, but *I'd* rather have seen her become a masseuse!

ANNETTE:

Do prospectors make so much money?

SUTTER:

(*Leaning expansively on the machine*)

Oh, don't waste your time feeling sorry for them, believe me. Of course, fortune may not come to them overnight. No. The really big money, skyrocket riches—that's the privilege of one man and one man only—the inventor!

ANNETTE:

(*Obviously intrigued by Sutter*)

Inventor of what?

SUTTER:

Of everything. You see these flippers? These bumpers? These luminous arrows? Well, they keep changing. And every day they're perfected. The players always ask for something new and the inventor always gives it to them.

MRS. DURANTY:

You mean all those little doodads mean money for the inventors?

SUTTER:

(*Laughing*)

And for Mrs. Duranty!

ARTHUR:

(*Very dryly, to Sutter*)

I think the young lady would like a return match.

SUTTER:

(*Gallantly stepping away from the machine*)

Her wish is my command.

(*To Annette*)

Please accept, dear young lady, these few free games I've won for you, and forgive me! Once I start talking, nothing can stop me. I know. It's often been pointed out to me, as if I never noticed it myself.

(*Pause*)

That's why the Old Man—the Old Man is my childhood friend; they call him that because he looks like an old man, though he's practically my own age. . . . How old would you say I am?

ANNETTE:

(*Laughing*)

I wouldn't. Ageless!

SUTTER:

Supposing I weren't ageless? How old would I be then?

ANNETTE:

Forty-five.

SUTTER:

Wrong! I haven't turned forty yet, but it's true that life has left its scars on me. Oh, if you knew my life—

ANNETTE:

(*Who has forgotten the machine*)

What's so special about your life?

SUTTER:

(*Sitting down to speak more comfortably*)
First of all, I served in the tropics and I caught malaria.
A terrible thing, malaria.

MRS. DURANTY:

(*Still behind the bar*)
They say you never get over diseases like that.

ANNETTE:

(*Sitting down beside Sutter and thereby provoking a furious exchange of signals between Arthur and Victor*)
I see. You were a . . . colonial prospector?

SUTTER:

That has nothing to do with it. I had decided to do my military service there, and all things considered, I don't regret it. Why? Because I had a horse. Ah, those trips across the desert—only a man and his horse beneath the burning sun!

(*Annette laughs.*)

ARTHUR:

(*Approaching Annette, followed by Victor who is trying to restrain him*)
Forgive me for butting in so "cavalierly" . . .

VICTOR:

(*Diplomatically*)
Listen, Arthur, just because we don't happen to like soldiers—

SUTTER:

Well, do you think I like them any better? Rather than

stay with them I chose . . .
(*Turning to Annette, mysteriously*)
What did I choose? To become a stevedore.

ANNETTE:

(*Laughing*)
A stevedore? Here? In the market?

SUTTER:

No, in Antwerp.

ARTHUR:

Of course.

MRS. DURANTY:

Do you know Antwerp, Mr. Sutter?

SUTTER:

After Antwerp, a strange period of my life began—no home, no job—and yet I didn't want either one. It was an experiment, something new, and I lived through it. But notice! I did it all quite consciously
(*Laughing*)
and temporarily! There's nothing wrong with being poor if you know when to stop.

VICTOR:

And if you want to. For instance, I'm not sure that little fellow who was in here just now . . .

ARTHUR:

I don't see what either of you have against . . .

ANNETTE:

Who are you talking about? I don't understand.

ARTHUR:

Well you see, Miss, just before you came in a rather nice-looking young fellow but poorly dressed and wearing a flower in his buttonhole . . .

ANNETTE:

(*Rushing to the bar*)

Really, Mrs. Duranty, how could you! Roger's been here and you didn't say a word about it! It's getting beyond endurance!

MRS. DURANTY:

(*Whining*)

No, I didn't tell you because my heart aches when I see you with that boy. Believe me, Annie. It's an old friend of your mother's who's talking to you, for your own good, Annie, for your own good . . .

ANNETTE:

Maybe you are, but I have to see him. I have to. Please excuse me.

(*As she leaves*)

Gentlemen!

(*Arthur and Victor are stupefied.*)

SUTTER:

(*Standing up*)

I've been here far too long myself. Young lady, you recall me to my duty. Permit me to accompany you: we'll take a few steps together and then separate, each to his own fate!

(*He picks up his briefcase*)

Sutter, quite banally, to the Corporation, and you . . .

(*He makes an expansive gesture*)

(*Annette leaves without answering. Sutter follows her after waving good-bye to everyone*)

MRS. DURANTY:

Poor little thing!

(*She counts over the coins left on the counter*)

ARTHUR:

(*Still standing, arms akimbo, in the middle of the stage*)
Incredible! She goes out to look for someone else and he forces himself on her.

VICTOR:

That ought to give you something to think about. If you want my opinion, she won't finish the evening with Mr. Roger.

ARTHUR:

What do you mean? You think that girl's stupid enough not to know an imposter when she sees one like that! He's obvious enough: Antwerp, the desert, the Corporation. . . . Besides, she was laughing.

VICTOR:

All the better. At least she wasn't bored, and besides, whatever you can say about the desert and the Corporation, he . . .

ARTHUR:

Listen, that guy's never set foot inside the Corporation except maybe to empty out that satchel. I could say I belong to a Corporation too.

VICTOR:

No, not the way you dress . . .

ARTHUR:

Mrs. Duranty, you know that man. Do you think he has an important position in the Corporation? Do you? Yes or no?

MRS. DURANTY:

All I know is, he's got more money than you boys.
(*She puts the money in a little bag and prepares to leave*)
Watch the bar a minute. If anyone comes, call me. I'll be upstairs.
(*Pointing to the machine*)
And don't shake her any more!
(*She exits*)

VICTOR:

You see? Mrs. Duranty's impressed by him because he has money. Maybe when you realize what money means to women you'll start trying to make some. And it's obvious you won't get rich everlastingly correcting papers for Universal Correspondence.

ARTHUR:

May I remind you that you aren't making any more than I am.

VICTOR:

No, but I will once I'm a doctor. And let me tell you, even with a scholarship, medical school has cost a lot of sacrifices and there'll probably be a lot more.

ARTHUR:

And you want me to get my degree just because you're getting yours? Well, I'm not going to, because I'd rather correct papers than waste my youth just so I can spend my Sundays when I'm seventy-seven playing billiards with some old colleague.
(*Pause*)
Do you have ten francs?

VICTOR:

I've already told you I don't.

ARTHUR:

Yes, you told me.

VICTOR:

Besides let me point out that we don't need any money:
(*Laughing*)
Sutter won five free games, dear Arthur, and they're all ours.

ARTHUR:

Listen, Victor, you may think I'm crazy, but I have no desire to pick up Sutter's crumbs. You can play if you want to, but under such conditions, I prefer being a spectator.

VICTOR:

It's up to you.
(*He gets ready to play*)

ARTHUR:

You're right, we'll be taking those damn games of his away from him.

(*Sneering*)

He sows, we reap. Turnabout . . .

(*Victor leans on the machine, resigned to listening to one of Arthur's speeches*)

Besides, he'd be only too happy for us not to take advantage of his winnings, you know he would!

(*Victor gestures evasively*)

And who cares whether Sutter would be happy or not? I'll start, if it's all right with you?

VICTOR:

You'll start? What a surprise.

(*He goes over to the bar and picks up the newspaper*)

ARTHUR:

(*Shaking the machine, which he has put out of order by playing too violently*)

Victor!

VICTOR:

What?

ARTHUR:

Victor, come here quick! Everything . . . everything's gone out!

VICTOR:

(*Approaching, the newspaper still in his hand*)

What did you do? You must have shaken her too hard, as usual.

ARTHUR:

No I didn't. No harder than usual . . . I can't understand

it, I just can't . . .

(*He shakes the machine again*)

VICTOR:

Listen, you've already broken her. There's no use making a complete wreck out of her now. Come on, we're not going to stay here and wait for Mrs. Duranty. You know what she's like. . . .

ARTHUR:

She should talk, with a machine like that!

VICTOR:

You can discuss your grievances with her some other time.

(*He takes Arthur's arm, but Arthur squirms free*)

ARTHUR:

(*Gazing at the machine*)

And the ball is still rolling on its own momentum even though it doesn't work. Nothing lights up, everything's jammed. Look!

VICTOR:

At what? The results of your prowess? Very interesting!

(*He pulls violently at Arthur's sleeve*)

ARTHUR:

I'm coming, I'm coming.

(*Darkness. Then two spotlights on Arthur and Victor standing downstage facing each other*)

Really, Victor, you act as though you thought I was crazy. I don't see why, unless I haven't made myself clear. . . . Now listen to me again.

(*Pause*)

What happens when you play and you happen to shake the machine a little? She breaks down and that's bad for everybody: The player's pride is wounded and naturally he gets annoyed; meanwhile the owner is deprived of a source of income. Now my system avoids both disadvantages, since all the player has to do is to put in another ten francs for the machine to start up again with a new game. That seems quite clear to me.

VICTOR:

Don't distort the problem. The idea's all right in itself, but I can't see any reason for the Corporation to put you in charge of improving its machines. You in particular, Arthur. And besides, where did you get your information from? From Sutter. And you've just spent hours demonstrating as clearly as 2 and 2 makes 4 that Sutter's only a third-rate employee putting on airs to seduce a girl someone else jilted.

ARTHUR:

Victor, I haven't changed my opinions regarding Sutter's personal position. I said and I still say that not only is he *not* the president's childhood friend, but that he never even *met* the president. Nevertheless, things aren't so simple as you'd like to think. For instance, there's one detail that Sutter couldn't have made up: the president's nickname—"the Old Man."

VICTOR:

All right. Even admitting the president should really be nicknamed "the Old Man," can you tell me how that will make it easier for us to get to see him?

(*Pause*)

Here's the situation. Old or not, we don't know this man and we have no way of getting in touch with him.

(*Sneering*)

Unless, of course, you count on Sutter's help.

ARTHUR:

Sutter's help! Victor, it's incredible. For once I have—we have—a real, concrete opportunity of getting rich together. Yet instead of thanking me, encouraging me, you set up a—a real barrage against me. I didn't ask for much. All I wanted was for you to come with me. . . . With two of us, we could have explained ourselves better, more clearly, more rationally. But since it bores you so much, let's forget it. I'll go by myself.

(*Arthur, suiting his actions to his words, is already disappearing. Victor, after a moment's hesitation, runs after him*)

SCENE TWO

(*The Old Man's Office. Somewhat stage left a desk behind which, enthroned in an armchair, is the Old Man, perhaps 50, rather a monster, a caricature of the Big Boss. He is nevertheless preyed upon by some sort of anxiety.*
Facing him across the desk somewhat stage right, so that the spectator sees them in profile, are Arthur and Victor. They have made an effort with regard to their wardrobe.)

THE OLD MAN:
Fantastic, the idea is simply fantastic: inspiring fear to increase pleasure.
(*Raising his arms*)
Now that's knowledge of the human heart for you. Ten francs, a twist of the wrist, and what you thought was finished, done, dead, revives, begins again!
(*Laughing*)
Like before, even better than before!

ARTHUR:
(*Leaning forward to speak*)
Please excuse me if I refer once again to the personal

experience I was just describing. But what can we talk about, after all, except what we've experienced personally? Well, as I said,

(*Laughing*)

confronted with this poor, unhappy machine, we had exactly . . . the same feeling . . .

VICTOR:

(*Trying to compensate for Arthur's enthusiasm, which he considers somewhat excessive*)

And we realized that the only means of restoring the incident to its normal proportions was to make it quite banal. In other words, so that by paying another ten francs . . .

THE OLD MAN:

Ten francs, what's that these days? A drink at the bar, nothing at all!

VICTOR:

That's exactly the line of thought we ourselves followed. For the player, a minimal expense, really quite insignificant; for the machine, a considerable gain, due to its frequent repetition.

ARTHUR:

Yes, but what we didn't know was that you would be as impressed as we were by the general value, I might say the human value, of this idea. Of course, we rather suspected you would be, that's why we came. But between suspecting and hoping, or to be quite frank, between wanting to hope and knowing, there's a great chasm. . . .

THE OLD MAN:

Now, now, if such ideas weren't immediately recognized and espoused by those in a position to bring them into the world, where would we be?

(*Pause*)

No, as far as I'm concerned, it's quite natural. But what surprises me, and above all what delights me, is to realize the enthusiasm each true discovery arouses among informed players, elite players.

(*Arthur and Victor stare at each other in astonishment*)

Oh, not that such things are miracles. The idea was in the air, everyone's been fumbling for it, but we had to find the formula. And what is that formula? A word, a single short decisive word: *Tilt*, suddenly appearing on the scoreboard to indicate: Disaster.

VICTOR:

(*Sitting up in his chair*)
Tilt!

ARTHUR:

(*Same business*)
But . . .

THE OLD MAN:

You too? You stumble over the word. What have you all got against English? Think it over before you decide. English speaks to the imagination. Our players will understand it and yet somehow, at the same time, not understand it.

ARTHUR:

It isn't . . .

THE OLD MAN:

You're young and perhaps patriotic as well. Think of it this way though. Take the Mass. Is the Mass said in French? And the Church knows what it's doing. The Church—what a businessman! And what a business! . . . But I'm getting needlessly excited . . .

(*Arthur evidently wants to speak but Victor plucks at his sleeve. Arthur obeys*)

(*To Victor*)

No, let him say what's on his mind. If he has objections, let's hear them. You came here to give your opinion, didn't you?

(*Arthur and Victor look at each other panic-stricken*)

I'm not the sort of man who believes in calling for a referendum every other minute, but between the questionnaire which is almost always filled out by imbeciles—who else would answer a survey but imbeciles?—and the living word, the direct exchange of ideas, I scarcely need to tell you there's a tremendous difference.

(*Pause*)

Nothing reassures me so much as having strangers, young men like yourselves, coming in to see us personally, coming to tell us they approve, or disapprove, or even, as in the present instance, that they simultaneously approve *and* disapprove the very scheme we're considering.

ARTHUR:

(Sitting up again)

What? Someone . . . already . . .

VICTOR:

(Riveted to his chair)

Ahead of us?

THE OLD MAN:

What?

(Pause)

Oh, I see. You thought you were the first . . .

(Laughs)

A misunderstanding! Our entire conversation rests on a misunderstanding. But that changes everything. Why the devil didn't you interrupt me? I know, I was off on one of my flights, but even so . . .

(Pause)

And here I was talking to you as if you were just ordinary players! Mass psychology! You must have thought I was some kind of an imbecile.

(Pause)

So you found it too. You discovered the trick.

(Laughing)

Death and resurrection, all for ten francs!

(He stands up, sits on the corner of the desk and claps Arthur on the shoulder)

ARTHUR:

(Stiffening)

Excuse me, but . . .

VICTOR:

(Trying to seem grown-up)
What did you expect, Arthur? We were fools *not* to have expected it. . . . Other people were working for the Corporation long before we . . .

THE OLD MAN:

(Standing up, to Victor)
Don't make yourself out tougher than you are. And besides, you have to understand your friend: he's disappointed, that's only natural; if my intuition doesn't deceive me, he's the one who had the idea in the first place.
(Sitting down again)
Ideas are money, and when you lose money, you lose heart too. Human, all too human!

ARTHUR:

I haven't lost heart but I am surprised; and believe me . . . not only . . . because we have to give up a profit we had every reason to anticipate, but also because . . . because I feel this coincidence is rather, well . . . let's say the word—*bizarre*. And if I didn't think so, it would be your turn to be surprised, since that would prove . . .

THE OLD MAN:

(Laughing)
So many surprises!
(Suddenly serious)
But I shouldn't laugh. I'm rather like you myself . . . Many things in this world surprise me too. You know, just this morning . . .

(*Pause*)

I sent for a report on operations in southern Italy, and you know, when I read it I was absolutely staggered. Now God knows I've seen Vesuvius smoking more than once. But all the same I never would have guessed that those people possessed, all in all, only two hundred and twenty machines! And what machines! Machines without flippers! Imagine that.

VICTOR:

I should think that was only natural, considering the standard of living on the one hand, and the climate on the other . . .

THE OLD MAN:

Natural! You think it's natural for a man to abandon himself to chance, natural to do without flippers voluntarily? Now take the Neapolitan fisherman then, does he put out to sea without oars?

(*For a moment now Arthur and Victor have been glancing at each other. Stage business: "Should we go?" Victor stands up.*)

Tired of listening to my speeches?

(*Sighing*)

Of course you have your problems and they don't have anything to do with mine. All right, leave if you want to. I won't keep you. Only promise to come back whenever you like. I feel we have things to tell one another.

(*He stands up and points at Arthur's forehead*)

Yes, there are things in there just waiting to come out, I'm sure of it.

VICTOR:

Are you coming, Arthur?

(*He takes his arm. Arthur shrugs him off.*)

ARTHUR:

(*To the Old Man*)

You're too kind, but we can't promise you anything. We all need a minimum of confidence to do our best and I must admit that today, when even that minimum . . . In other words, when something you've pinned all your hopes on fails, and what's more fails without your even knowing how and why, you start thinking—even if there are no facts to prove it—that the next scheme . . . You should understand, yes, you particularly, considering your position, how it is . . . how the mind works this way.

(*He takes Victor's arm, ready to leave now*)

Are you coming, Victor?

THE OLD MAN:

(*Approaching Victor and Arthur*)

Suit yourselves. But let me remind you, my friends, a return visit isn't so difficult. One little phone call does the trick.

(*Laughing, his arms around Arthur's and Victor's shoulders*)

The bureaucratic labyrinth? A myth invented by weaklings. The president of a corporation isn't the lord of a manor whose name you know only because you happened to get lost once when you were on his property. . . . He's a man like anyone else, a man you can go and see, a man you can say anything to whenever you feel the need . . . Consequently . . .

(Arthur and Victor, the Old Man's arms still around their shoulders, look at each other in astonishment and suddenly struggle free. They want to leave, but do not go)

All right then, agreed? Whenever you get an idea, you run in and see us. . . . If I'm not here, it doesn't matter, you can always talk to my secretary. You can tell him anything.

(Laughing)

He's my other self. Besides,

(Pause)

here he is now.

(Enter Mr. Roger, transformed, elegant: his trousers impeccably pressed and a flower still in his buttonhole)

(Sitting down again)

Roger, I'd like you to meet two of our co-workers. These young men have restored my confidence in the next generation . . .

(Laughing)

yours, that is. At least you're not all loafers.

(To Arthur and Victor)

He's not an enthusiast of great intellectual efforts.

MR. ROGER:

(With a short impertinent laugh)

That's right, Constantine. I don't like to work but I'm perfectly willing that other people should.

(The Old Man laughs indulgently and claps Mr. Roger on the shoulder. Mr. Roger sits down on a corner of the desk. Arthur and Victor, transfixed for a moment, question each other in sign language, particularly astonished by Roger's behavior)

THE OLD MAN:

(To Arthur and Victor)

You see, it's not hard to get along here. We're very understanding, a regular Liberty Hall. So now that you know the way . . .

(He dismisses them and turns smiling toward Mr. Roger. Arthur and Victor exit like sleepwalkers.

Darkness. Then two spotlights on Arthur and Victor, who exchange all their remarks as they walk, stop, start again, etc.)

VICTOR:

Arthur, please, stop interpreting. What else do you expect? When a boy who just last week was almost a bum suddenly turns into the president's secretary and "friend," I don't think there can be much doubt . . . The subject is closed.

ARTHUR:

Yes, it's insane, but . . . I'd still like to try and find out . . . how it happens that this Mr. Roger . . . and so quickly . . .

VICTOR:

Oh, it's the classic case. You act like a Bohemian up to a point, but one fine day your family gets worried. 'We've got to find something for the boy to do.' Nothing could be easier. Papa's a stockholder in a Corporation . . . *You* figure out the rest.

ARTHUR:

All right. But how can all that—family decision, pulling strings, hiring the secretary—have happened? . . .

VICTOR:

Look, we don't know exactly what his situation was last week. It's perfectly possible he's been working as an apprentice for a long time now and that he plays at being a vagabond in his spare time—to seduce romantic young ladies, if you know who I mean.

ARTHUR:

Yes, but in that case Annette wouldn't have been so excited about him, at least not if she's as romantic as you think. And besides, Sutter would have recognized him. Unless of course, as I always suspected, Sutter never set . . .

VICTOR:

So according to you, what we saw at Mrs. Duranty's was one man who boasted about being the Old Man's friend and who wasn't, and another who happened to be his secretary, the Old Man's secretary, and who didn't choose to say so. It's sheer madness!

ARTHUR:

(*Pensive*)

And besides, they might have pretended . . . not to know each other . . . but that's unlikely.

(*Pause*)

Even so, with someone like Sutter . . .

(*Pause*)

Only if I find out that my idea, an idea that meant an absolutely unhoped-for opportunity for us, has been stolen . . . stolen by . . .

VICTOR:

Arthur, I can see what's going on in your mind.

ARTHUR:

I'm not saying anything, but you'll have to admit there's something peculiar all the same . . . and that we've every reason to make . . . certain suppositions.

VICTOR:

But not *that* one. Don't you remember that by the time we thought of the idea, Sutter had already left?

ARTHUR:

So?

VICTOR:

So you'd better do something about your persecution complex.

(*Pause*)

And while you're at it, suppose Mr. Roger got his job with the Old Man . . .

ARTHUR:

The Old Man! I wonder why he asked us to come back? I've got my suspicions. You ask people from outside to come see you, they bring you their ideas quite trustingly, and what happens? A few months later someone else is making money out of them. . . . God knows who. It's really disgraceful.

(*Pause*)

You're right, we won't go back there again.

SCENE THREE

(*The Turkish Bath. Stage left, the service window: towels, soap, etc. Near the window, a basket; stage right, a bench. Mrs. Duranty is sitting behind the window.*
Enter stage left Sutter, adjusting his tie, a towel over his shoulder.)

SUTTER:

You better check your plugs, Mrs. Duranty. A little more current and it would have been the electric chair for Sutter. Trust your friends to do you in!

(*He laughs and tosses his towel into the basket*)

MRS. DURANTY:

I know. The current goes the wrong way, but what can I do about it? What an inspiration it was to give up my little Gayety for this miserable Turkish bath! And you can believe me, Mr. Sutter, I've sent for the electrician three times. I do my duty—not like you, Mr. Sutter. Despite all your promises, my machine still hasn't come. I knew I should have suspected something, with that awful "Tilt." Whenever the customers see that word they lose their heads and start kicking everything, and then they go

away. A fine invention! Whoever thought of that . . .
(*Pause*)
And you promised to have it fixed for me in two days.

SUTTER:

Amazing.

MRS. DURANTY:

Yes, amazing is the word, all right. And you're supposed
to make it blow hot and cold at the Corporation. It looks
like all *you're* interested in was finding a job for Mr.
Roger.

(*For a moment now Arthur and Victor have been standing
in the doorway at stage right, glancing at each other dumbfounded.*)

Imagine giving a job like that to a good-for-nothing just
because he knows English! After all!

(*Arthur and Victor hesitate and then approach Mrs. Duranty*)

SUTTER:

(*Delighted by the diversion*)
Well, my friends, how's it going? I hope as well for you
as it is for Sutter, which is as well as it *can* go when you've
got a mountain of work looming up ahead of you and not
time enough to reach the summit.
(*Pause*)
And how are your deals going? Not so good, I suppose.
Well, times are hard. Still, you both speak English pretty
well and English is the Open Sesame of the modern world.

(*Pause, then to Arthur*)
You give English lessons, don't you?

ARTHUR:

I'm sorry to contradict you, but as it hapens I've never taught English. Besides, I'm only teaching temporarily, thank God.

VICTOR:

And just between us, I'm afraid you're overestimating its importance. And no matter how valuable English is, I could scarcely agree that the first imbecile to come along is capable of taking over . . .

SUTTER:

You've put your finger on it—I couldn't agree with you more! But how did you find out I got the little fellow into the Corporation? Mrs. Duranty, I suspect you've been chattering—whenever your afflictions give you a chance. Ah, frivolity, see where you lead us!

(*Enter Annette stage left, her hair wet, a towel in her hand. Arthur and Victor nudge each other*)

ANNETTE:

(*As soon as she sees Sutter, furiously*)
Lord, you're not hard to find, even without looking!

SUTTER:

(*Embarrassed*)
Annette! How strange fate is. There we were, washing ourselves not two steps away from each other and nothing, nothing, gave us a clue. . . .

(*Reproachfully*)
Mrs. Duranty . . .

MRS. DURANTY:

So you see she's not such a chatterbox as all that, Mrs. Duranty!

ANNETTE:

(*To Sutter*)
Anyway, my dear, let me tell you that as far as I'm concerned, a broken promise . . .

SUTTER:

Have mercy, these hot-headed young men have already appointed themselves judges to consign your unfortunate friend . . .

ANNETTE:

(*To Arthur and Victor, who have been left behind by these remarks*)
So you've had dealings with this gentleman too, have you? Well, I pity you!

ARTHUR:

(*Hurriedly*)
No, no, we ran into him quite accidentally. We just happened to stop by Mrs. Duranty's to see if her machine . . .

SUTTER:

There's no need to rub salt in Mrs. Duranty's wounds!
(*Laughs*)

MRS. DURANTY:

It's no laughing matter, Mr. Sutter.

SUTTER:

Impatient as a girl!

ANNETTE:

Ordinary mortals might be less impatient if a certain person didn't lure them into the supernatural world of lightning success.

(*Sutter throws up his hands and begins walking back and forth, gesticulating. Arthur and Victor are boiling over.*)

ARTHUR:

(*Boldly approaching Annette*)
You'll probably . . . I'm afraid . . . you'll think I'm being indiscreet, but I can tell, or at least I think I can, that . . . that something serious is bothering you, something urgent . . . It's because I've always thought of you as . . .

VICTOR:

Don't talk nonsense, Arthur. Just because we saw her calmly playing the machine once . . .

ANNETTE:

In any case, you won't have many chances to see that attractive spectacle again.

MRS. DURANTY:

(*To Arthur and Victor*)
Annette's not like you. When Mrs. Duranty doesn't have her machine . . .

ARTHUR:

(*To Annette*)
Really . . . you . . . don't play any more? At all? Because . . .

ANNETTE:

Ask Sutter why I don't feel like playing any more.

(*Mrs. Duranty dozes off. Arthur and Victor glance at one another and approach Sutter whom they nevertheless do not dare question. Sutter stops walking when he hears Annette say his name.*)

SUTTER:

(*Brushing Victor and Arthur away as if they were flies*)
Look, Annette, try to understand me. Make an effort. I could have mentioned you, of course I could. A hundred times, a thousand times. But I know my man, the life he leads, I see the mad dance of ideas in his head. You have to know how to wait in ambush for the right moment, the great moment, the fatal moment!
(*Pause*)
I ask you—is it so hard to be patient for five weeks? Or even ten, since now you know you'll be able to leave that movie house of yours?

ANNETTE:

Better yet! Now it's not just days any more, it's weeks!

VICTOR:

(*Getting his courage up*)
It's obvious the lady has observed in the circle of her immediate acquaintances a certain skyrocket ascent . . .

SUTTER:

Such big words for such little things.

ARTHUR:

If you ask me, pleasure and success . . .

SUTTER:

Ah, success, or rather the notion of it people have these days—there's public enemy number one.

(*To Annette*)

Where is true success but in communication, feeling yourself near others, reading their thoughts, foreseeing their destiny—yes, Annette . . .

(*Arthur and Victor betray a common impulse of discouragement*)

ANNETTE:

You're awfully pleased with yourself.

SUTTER:

Wrong move! I didn't say I always triumph where others fail. Sometimes I too, alas! . . .

(*In a lower voice*)

I had a son once, we were fond of each other, we understood each other, we used to take walks in the country; well, when that son of mine was fourteen, he was drowned. It happened in Switzerland—in Lake Leman.

MRS. DURANTY:

(*Awakening briefly from her nap*)

Fourteen! Poor little thing. I was sick once at Vevey . . . And there I was living in Lausanne without suspecting anything.

ANNETTE:

I hope you'll forgive me, but your Swiss sorrows leave me quite indifferent.

(*Arthur and Victor laugh and whisper to one another*)

SUTTER:

Annette, once more you misunderstand me. If I've re-
called this sad event, it was merely so you would know
that even Sutter has his weaknesses.

(*Annette, Arthur and Victor laugh*)

(*Approaching Arthur and Victor aggressively*)

Still hot-headed, you two! Nevertheless, I remember a
certain day—you were with us, Annette—when that im-
petuosity . . . But that's another sad recollection. I'm
sorry.

(*Pause*)

Let me give you some advice all the same, young men:
When the machine resists, don't be in such a hurry to
accuse the machine. Ask yourselves instead if you haven't
forgotten a wheel somewhere. I don't know . . .

(*Clapping Arthur on the shoulder*)

maybe the top flippers.

ARTHUR:

(*An outburst*)

That's . . . that's not going to be where we concentrate,
and maybe one of these days . . .

(*Victor prudently plucks at Arthur's jacket*)

SUTTER:

One of these days? What does that mean? Live in the
present. Damn it, at least try!

(*With a deep sigh*)

That's what I do.

ANNETTE:

You maybe, but not me. And since I have no predilection for the role of the obliging victim hoaxed by the wicked gentleman . . .

(*She indicates she is about to leave. Bewildered, Arthur and Victor show no reaction at all*)

SUTTER:

Then you don't trust me any more, Annette? And why not? Just because I don't keep the people I'm doing favors for up to date on how things stand with them? Well, those aren't my methods. I don't . . .

(*He is about to run stage right to head off Annette who, however, does not move*)

ANNETTE:

Don't be angry with me. Maybe I lost my temper a little, (*Pause*)

but I was only trying to make you understand . . .

Listen . . . maybe if we tried explaining to each other . . . clearly, calmly. Let's go somewhere and talk, all right?

SUTTER:

Annette's wish is Sutter's command!

(*Arthur's and Victor's gestures grow increasingly distressed*)

ANNETTE:

See you soon, Mrs. Duranty. Gentlemen . . .

SUTTER:

Until next time, Mrs. Duranty!

MRS. DURANTY:

(*Waking up*)

Bye, bye, Annie dear. You won't forget me, Mr. Sutter, will you?

SUTTER:

A promise is a promise!

(*Then turning around to Arthur and Victor*)

Good luck, my friends, and watch out for those flippers.

(*He exits behind Annette stage right*)

ARTHUR:

(*Trembling with rage*)

That's . . . that's the limit! How dare he? You're not going to tell me this time . . .

VICTOR:

No more speeches now. That's enough for today. And besides, you know what it is. He's invented a system: step on the little fellow to impress the girls. He's got her where he wants her now. She needs him, so . . .

ARTHUR:

Needs him?

(*To Mrs. Duranty*)

Really, Mrs. Duranty, how could you let a girl like that, a girl you're genuinely fond of, count on a . . .

MRS. DURANTY:

I count on him too. And besides, ever since Annette took it into her head to get work as a prospector . . .

ARTHUR:

A prospector!

VICTOR:

Poor child! Still, she certainly has connections. For instance, she could always go see her friend Mr. Roger at the Corporation . . .

MRS. DURANTY:

You're all breaking my eardrums with your Corporation. (*Laughing*)
Maybe you want to go there too?

ARTHUR:

No, we don't want to go there. But strange as it may seem to you, we've been there.

(*Victor plucks at Arthur's sleeve*)

MRS. DURANTY:

(*Laughing*)
A fine looking pair of businessmen you'd make!
(*The sound of running water off-stage*)
There, it's starting again! That hot-water faucet's always giving me trouble!
(*She exits stage left, muttering*)

ARTHUR:

Of course, for her the Corporation is Sutter. Still, I'm not dreaming, am I? We went there without going through Sutter.

(*Discouraged*)
When I think that he'll never know . . .
(*He collapses on the bench*)

VICTOR:

(*Sitting down beside Arthur*)
It's a good thing, because then he'd find out what happened at that interview and I scarcely need tell you it's results that count for him, *immediate results.*

ARTHUR:

(*Suddenly standing up, as though propelled by a spring, and parodying Sutter*)
"Live in the present, damn it" and what a present! The top flippers!
(*Pause, then bursting into laughter*)
Oh, Victor!

VICTOR:

(*Standing up*)
Have you gone crazy?

ARTHUR:

(*Laughing still harder*)
No, no. Just the opposite. Victor, I've got an idea.
(*He laughs so hard he can scarcely speak*)
Since he likes those top flippers so much, our Mr. Sutter, you know what we're going to do? We're going to get rid of them for good!

VICTOR:

What're you talking about?

ARTHUR:

(*Provocatively*)

What am I talking about? An idea, just another idea. Still, what have we got to lose? The Old Man . . .

VICTOR:

You mean you're serious? You want . . . to go back there? . . .

SCENE FOUR

(The Shoe Store. At first we see only Arthur and Victor. They are both walking, but in opposite directions. When they meet, they speak: sometimes, however, one speaks while the other is walking, etc. Victor is wearing a new coat; Arthur, a light-colored scarf.)

VICTOR:

Yes, he took it. Yes, he paid for it. And I'm as pleased about it as you are, believe me. But I still don't consider a bad idea a good one just because the Old Man liked it. *(Pause)*
I still maintain—against anyone and anything—that getting rid of those top flippers was sheer madness.

ARTHUR:

Listen, Victor, you know me. You know I'm not likely to worship success for its own sake. But use your head, please. Don't you think that if the Old Man, who knows the machine better than all of us, was attracted by my proposition, it was because it seemed satisfactory to him? Objectively satisfactory. And don't tell me he was letting himself be talked into it. I may have certain persuasive

abilities, but with a man like that . . . No, I spoke to him
very objectively. And he understood, as you should, that
in a well-balanced machine the bottom flippers are strong
enough to send the ball all the way to the top so that
even without the top flippers the player is never reduced
to passivity. He may have to wait longer, of course, but
it's a thrilling wait, because he watches not only . . .

VICTOR:

Now look, Arthur, I'll be just as well off if you spare me
the complete version of the speech I heard quite clearly
back in the Old Man's office.

ARTHUR:

Oh, you were listening to what I was saying? Well, that's
a surprise. You know, I had the distinct impression you
were getting rather bored with me. You were really much
too busy contradicting Mr. Roger and bothering him to
pay much attention to anything else. Besides, I wonder
what gives you the . . .

VICTOR:

Forgive me. I forgot that anyone dear to the lady of your
thoughts automatically becomes an object of your respect.

ARTHUR:

Don't talk nonsense. I have no particular respect for that
young man but on the other hand, we have no reason to
be angry with him. He knows his place, he listens to what
you say, he never tries to put himself forward . . . and if
everyone else behaved the way he does . . .

VICTOR:

Don't mince words, Arthur. I'm perfectly aware that when you say "everyone else" you mean Sutter, and I must admit I'm beginning to worry a little about your sanity. After all, it's not quite natural that Sutter's mere existence . . .

ARTHUR:

An existence which doesn't make much of a show at the Corporation. You'll have to admit that. You must have noticed—I have—that we've never seen him there. I know we've only gone twice and there's no positive . . .
(*He stumbles*)

VICTOR:
What's the matter?

ARTHUR:
(*Picking up his shoe*)
I've just lost my sole.

(*Victor laughs until Arthur begins laughing too: they are friends again*)

You see, it's not so bad having a little money, after all.
(*Pause*)
What would you say if I decided to treat myself to a new pair of shoes?

VICTOR:
I couldn't encourage you enough. But for God's sake, don't buy them just anywhere.

(*Darkness. When the lights come on, we are in a shoe store:* *a few chairs and some boxes on the floor. Arthur, sitting at* *stage left, holds out his shoeless foot on the little stool where* *Annette, now selling shoes, is sitting. Victor sits on another* *chair, next to Arthur.*)

ARTHUR:

(*While Annette is lacing up another shoe*)

What amazes me most, you know, is the way these things are connected. Of course, I believe in the law of succession and all that just as much as anyone else, maybe more than anyone else. For instance, I'm absolutely convinced that one piece of luck leads to another. It was quite obvious this morning: right after our victory, it occurred to me that if I went to see Mrs. Duranty I would probably run into you. And then, I don't know why, I just had an urge to buy some shoes.

(*Annette and Victor laugh*)

Oh, I don't claim to have second sight . . .

VICTOR:

I'm glad to hear you say it. The truth is you were as stupefied as I was to find Miss Annette in this store.

ARTHUR:

Of course. No one in the world could have guessed . . .

ANNETTE:

(*Standing up*)

Do you know that you're both fantastic? Why shouldn't an usherette become a salesgirl if she wants to? After all, you changed *your* jobs, and quite spectacularly too: you joined the Corporation without firing a shot, made them listen to you, got a contract . . .

VICTOR:

(*Standing*)

I'm afraid you haven't quite understood what we mean, Miss Annette. No change is very surprising in itself; and besides we already knew you were thinking of leaving your former position. It's just that we thought . . . we were under the impression you wanted to . . .

ANNETTE:

Oh, you're still talking about the Sutter period. God, how far away that is.

(*Laughing*)

As a matter of fact, didn't that handsome caballero have something to do . . .

ARTHUR:

(*Suddenly standing up, one shoe off*)

Sutter! Don't be ridiculous.

(*He sits down again*)

VICTOR:

No, we don't owe anything to Sutter or to anyone else. We got into the Corporation on our own.

(*He sits down again*)

ANNETTE:

Well, you certainly were lucky.

(*She sits down on her stool again*)

ARTHUR:

(*While Annette offers him another shoe*)
Lucky? Well, luckier than if we had asked the "handsome cabellero" for anything.

(*Annette and Arthur laugh*)

VICTOR:

You two are really something. Sutter's impossible, I agree there, but all the same he's proved that in certain cases...

(*Enter Mr. Roger stage right*)

MR. ROGER:

I hope I'm not interrupting you, Annie.

(*Arthur and Victor stupefied*)

ANNETTE:

Of course not, Roger. I'm delighted to see you. I didn't expect ... I'll be with you in a minute.
(*To Arthur, whom she wishes to get rid of quickly*)
You'll take these then, isn't that right?

ARTHUR:

Actually, I wonder if ... if I don't prefer the others. You know, the first ones ...

(*Annette looks for the box*)

MR. ROGER:

(*Sitting down, to Annette*)
There's no hurry. I've got plenty of time. I don't have to keep strict hours, thank God.

ARTHUR:

(*After Victor nudges him, to Mr. Roger*)
You see, our meeting this morning has led to ...

(*He indicates the shoe on one of his feet. Mr. Roger smiles very slightly*)
our meeting this evening. If. Mr. Constantine and you hadn't . . . it's likely I never . . . anyway, not today . . .

VICTOR:

(*To Arthur, but for Mr. Roger's benefit*)
No, I'm not sure this conversation . . .
(*To Mr. Roger*)
I just happened to be explaining to my friend that if the Corporation expects regular cooperation from us, we must have a contract here and now . . .

MR. ROGER:

I'm sorry, but I've made it a rule never to talk business except at the office.
(*Raising his voice, to Annette*)
You be my witness, Annette. I don't let myself be eaten up by my social obligations.

(*Victor sits down, furious. Annette returns carrying a box*)

ANNETTE:

(*To Arthur*)
These are the ones, I think.
(*To Mr. Roger*)
It was nice of you to come and see me . . .
(*Smiling*)
ahead of time.

MR. ROGER:

Actually, Annie, I came to give you a little talking-to.

ANNETTE:

I . . . I don't see why. My request had nothing very un-
usual about it.

(*Arthur and Victor prick up their ears*)

MR. ROGER:

Really, do you see me, *me*, insisting to Mr. Constantine
(*Laughing*)
that he have a machine repaired
(*Scornfully*)
on credit? Of course, he'd agree, but I have no desire to
get into that world of favors offered and services rendered
. . . I don't like bookkeeping in general, and that kind! . . .

ANNETTE:

Why don't you just say you didn't want to do anything
for Mrs. Duranty? That would be nearer the truth and it
would hurt my feelings less.

MR. ROGER:

I've nothing against the lady. It's just that she's always
managed to annoy me. Her continual ecstasies over the
machine . . .
(*He laughs slightly*)

ANNETTE:

But if the machines bother you so much, Roger, what are
you doing at the Corporation? You might have found a
thousand other ways of using your talents and making a
place for yourself in society.

MR. ROGER:

Don't be ridiculous, Annie. You know perfectly well how it happened.

ANNETTE:

Go on. You don't become someone's private secretary just to win a bet with Sutter.

(*Arthur and Victor exchange an extravagant series of gestures*)

And besides the whole business sounds shady to me.
(*Imitating Mr. Roger*)
"I accept under certain conditions. I come when I can, I leave when I want to. I don't worry about anything." That kind of talk doesn't convince any boss, no matter how charming the employee is, or how good at jabbering English. Try that on someone else, Mr. Roger!

MR. ROGER:

I suppose the Old Man had his reasons, Annie.
(*He is about to leave*)

ANNETTE:

Oh yes, mysterious reasons for recruiting his staff from young men who know nothing at all about the machine.

MR. ROGER:

Now how do you know I haven't served my apprenticeship meanwhile?

ANNETTE:

Really? You managed that too?

(*Laughing*)
You deigned to make appearances in cafes, *you*? No, how stupid I am! They have pinball arcades now, don't they —excellent for novices in need of training! You can even choose your machine! If it isn't going so well with one, you can always try another.
(*Tearing the flower Mr. Roger is still wearing out of his buttonhole and sobbing*)
But don't go dressed like that. People might look at you peculiarly. The clientele in those places!

(*Mr. Roger, quite dignified, picks up his flower and exits stage right. Annette sits down on her stool and cries, her head in her hands. Arthur and Victor, who have followed the whole scene bewildered and impotent, consult each other with looks and gestures: should they approach Annette?*)

ARTHUR:

I'm sorry. Perhaps we should leave you by yourself, but it seems to me—I may be wrong—but in such circumstances it's really better to speak. Oh, I don't want to try to console you, but I know from experience that at the moment there's always a tendency to overestimate the seriousness . . .

VICTOR:

(*Standing up, to Arthur*)
I don't care what you say . . . It's not hard to imagine that in a case like that . . .

ANNETTE:

(*Raising her head*)
I'm sorry—making a scene like that. And I've always hated people who make scenes . . .

ARTHUR:

We must have seemed awfully cowardly . . . We should have intervened, said something . . . but how could we make you understand . . . Our situation at the . . .

VICTOR:

(*To Arthur*)
What are you trying to say?
(*To Annette*)
The truth is we didn't know enough to be able to help you. It's not enough to know that Mrs. Duranty's machine . . .

ANNETTE:

(*Standing up, roughly*)
Who's talking about Mrs. Duranty! Don't you understand anything?

VICTOR:

Not much, as a matter of fact. But all you have to do is explain . . .

ANNETTE:

There's nothing to explain, except that I'm tired of putting up with these people's insults all the time. The machine? I know more about it than they do and they put on airs because I happened to ask for a miserable job as a prospector.

(*Annette sits down on her stool and begins crying once more*)

ARTHUR:

It's all the more unforgivable since you're hardly the sort of person who asks for a job she's not equipped to handle. And then, it's enough to have seen you once . . . You talk about the machine with such passion . . .

VICTOR:

(*To Arthur*)

Its not passion that counts but intelligence. Now it happens that Miss . . .

ANNETTE:

(*Raising her head*)

But I'm not passionate and I'm not intelligent. I know how to use my eyes, that's all. And not only on the machine, the players too.

(*Standing up*)

If those gentlemen were willing to consult my humble opinion, I might be able to give them some valuable information. For instance, I could inform them that *right now* the players happen to be extremely dissatisfied.

ARTHUR:

Dissatisfied? You think so? Why? . . .

VICTOR:

The important thing, you understand, would be to know on just what point . . .

ANNETTE:

No, it's the principle itself! As a matter of fact, it *is* ridiculous: you play, you try to understand, and you never know where you are, whether you're winning or losing, if you've still a chance left or no chance at all . . .

VICTOR:

Let's not exaggerate. There's a very simple way of following the game: watching the numbers that light up on the scoreboard. If the player doesn't know how to read the numbers . . .

ARTHUR:

The numbers! You're forgetting that sometimes he doesn't even have time to look at them.
(*Turning toward Annette*)
Yes, I've noticed it myself. Sometimes it's hard to watch the game and the scoreboard at the same time. . . . You look up . . .

ANNETTE:

Yes, but the number's already gone. And now there's another one there, and then it disappears too, before you even have time to read it.
(*She sits down on the chair stage left; then meaningfully*)
No, what the scoreboard needs is pictures. That's what anyone will tell you.

VICTOR:

I never heard anything like that. And I must say that even though I'm a regular player I never thought of it before.

ARTHUR:

Neither have I, up until now. But I did have a vague feel-

ing that something wasn't, well . . . that something was
missing . . .
(*Pause. He thinks for a minute*)
Maybe a concrete image, something striking.

ANNETTE:
(*Standing up and approaching Arthur*)
And pleasant to look at, something that gives you a notion
of just where you are at the same time.

ARTHUR:
(*Still standing, after a long pause, striking his forehead*)
A rocket, a moon!

VICTOR:
(*Indignant*)
The moon?

ARTHUR:
A moon and a rocket. Yes.
(*Pause. He reflects for a moment*)
And when the rocket reaches the moon then . . .

ANNETTE:
(*Laughing, excitedly*)
Then?

ARTHUR:
(*Suddenly*)
Then the moon will light up.

ANNETTE:
(*Leaning coquettishly toward Arthur*)
And when it lights up?

ARTHUR:

(*After a pause, reflecting*)
That means you'll get a free game.

ANNETTE:

(*Laughing*)
That's not bad.

VICTOR:

(*Furious*)
Excuse me for cutting short your euphoria, Arthur, but as far as I'm concerned, your idea seems quite childish, to say the least.

ANNETTE:

(*To Victor*)
I suppose that for a superior breed of man like you, the game is just an arithmetic lesson. But what do you think people want? They want to have fun!

(*Victor begins walking up and down, his hands in his pockets. He makes a great show of his disdain*)

ARTHUR:

(*After a pause, reflecting*)
There'll be two rockets. One that's stationary, the observer-rocket, and another that rises each time the score increases, getting closer . . .

(*Annette moves closer to Arthur and puts her hand on his shoulder*)

Until it finally reaches the moon . . .

ANNETTE:

(*Taking Arthur's hand*)
Which immediately lights up.

ARTHUR:

(*Flattered and pleased, holding Annette's hand in his*)
So, between the two rockets, the distance would grow
progressively greater . . .

ANNETTE:

(*Her face closer to Arthur's and with a voluptuous smile*)
While between the second rocket and the moon, on the
contrary . . .
(*She laughs*)
Is that right?

ARTHUR:

(*In ecstasies, laughing*)
Of course that's right. Absolutely right!
(*Suddenly serious*)
You know, Annette, that's a wonderful idea I . . . we've
just had.
(*Turning to Victor who has stopped a certain distance
away and followed the scene sneering*)
And I'm almost sure, Victor, that if we propose it to the
Old Man . . .

(*Victor doesn't budge*)

(*Returns to Annette*)
Yes, I think so! Annette, it's now or never. This is our
chance to talk to him about you!

SCENE FIVE

(*The Old Man's Office. The Old Man is sitting in his armchair. At stage left Mr. Roger, standing, with papers in his
hand. Sitting slightly to the right, as in scene two, Victor
and Arthur.*)

THE OLD MAN:

(*Standing up and pounding his fist on the desk, to Mr.
Roger*)

Drop the pinball arcades, is that your formula?

(*Mr. Roger lowers his head a little*)

Only you're forgetting one thing: there happens to be a
quota, a quota I've got to keep up all by myself. And now
that the better places are getting rid of their machines,
this is the time you . . . I suppose you haven't read this?

(*He takes a paper off his desk and reads:*)

"The customers at the tables complain that the noisy
games at the bar . . ." The customers at the tables! How
many Mr. Rogers are there?

MR. ROGER:

I'm afraid you're dramatizing the situation a little. . . . It's
not because a few establishments . . .

THE OLD MAN:

Even if there were only one! It's the first one that counts. Haven't you learned that yet?

(*Mr. Roger exits without a word stage left*)

Yes, go on, you'd better get out of my sight.

(*With a sigh*)

Hopeless!

(*Walking up and down, to Arthur and Victor, who have been listening with a mixture of terror and pleasure*)

You see what we've come to: the customers at the tables making the laws, and with what justification? Is it the tables who bring in the cash? No. It's always the bar. Everywhere!

VICTOR:

(*Advancing toward the Old Man*)

It's obvious that . . . that if you got rid of the machines you'd cut down business at the bar right away.

THE OLD MAN:

(*Suddenly turning around*)

It's staring them right in the face, but just try explaining it to them!

(*He continues walking*)

ARTHUR:

(*Following the Old Man and followed by Victor who would like to speak but doesn't dare*)

Yes, its always hard to make people understand what's really staring them right in the face, to use your expression. Nonetheless, I'm convinced they'll be forced to ac-

knowledge the bar's indisputable preponderance, once the
interest aroused by the machine is even greater, more
violent, more constant than it is today. But for that to
happen the machine must become a center of attraction,
not only for the player but for the spectator too. That's
why the plan I submitted to you—merely an outline, of
course—corresponds so well to the new requirements
we're talking about. . . . As a matter of fact, the spectator's
possibility of following the game's progress over the player's shoulder arouses a general and spontaneous move-
ment of infallible advantage to the machine. As I think
I've explained to you, the rocket, taking off . . .

SUTTER:
(*Offstage*)
Constantine! Constantine!

(*The Old Man, beside himself, sits down at his desk and
pretends to be working. Arthur and Victor are thunder-
struck.*)

(*Rushing in stage right*)
I knew you were here.
(*Pointing somewhere*)
And he tried to stop me getting in. I broke through the
blockade.
(*Pause*)
You're busy, I see, but I only want a minute of your time,
a question of life or death.

THE OLD MAN:
I'm sorry, Sutter, but as a mater of fact, I am very busy.

(*Indicating his papers*)

I haven't time to talk to you.

SUTTER:

I don't want you to talk to me, I want you to listen. A minute—a half-minute. All I want is a half-minute of your time.

THE OLD MAN:

(*Resigned*)

How much do you need?

SUTTER:

Well, since we can't see each other any more except in public . . .

(*To Arthur and Victor*)

Good morning, gentlemen. . . . Fifteen thousand. Yes, fifteen thousand minimum.

THE OLD MAN:

Fifteen thousand!

SUTTER:

Let me explain. Evelyn is sick, seriously sick. Hospital! Emergency! Her husband? Gone. Exactly. Left! Last Thursday! Like a coward! Again, Sutter saw it coming.

THE OLD MAN:

I don't have fifteen thousand francs just like that.

SUTTER:

Maybe not on you, but you could get them. I'll wait. An hour, two hours, if I have to. I've burned my bridges, you know I have. A mistake maybe, but Sutter has his pride, like anyone else.

THE OLD MAN:

(*Taking out his wallet*)

Here. At least this will keep you seeing what's coming.

SUTTER:

Give me another thousand. You have it—I saw it.

THE OLD MAN:

I can't now, but . . . Come another time, if you have to. Tomorrow, the day after . . . I don't know.

SUTTER:

Tomorrow? You don't know what you're saying. Sickness moves fast.

THE OLD MAN:

(*Standing up, his two hands flat on the desk*)

Not a penny more. You'll not get a penny more from me.

SUTTER:

All right, I'm going. Thanks all the same.

(*Turning when he reaches the door*)

I'm counting on you. Until tomorrrow then . . . tomorrow.

(*Exits*)

THE OLD MAN:

(*Sighing, to Arthur and Victor who have difficulty getting control of themselves*)

Now you see my fatal destiny.

(*Wiping off his forehead*)

What a day!

(*Pause*)

Well, you were saying just now—please go on. Where were you?

ARTHUR:

(*Standing up*)

At . . . at the rocket . . . I was saying that given the principle of progression through space, my objective: the moon . . .

THE OLD MAN:

Not again! What are you trying to get at with this business of the moon . . . and the rocket?

ARTHUR:

That's just what I was going to tell you. . . . Since the spectators can observe the player's progress, they feel they are concerned, involved . . . and the mere fact of seeing it clearly . . .

THE OLD MAN:

Seeing clearly! And the two of you came here to tell me about a thing like that!

(*He begins walking again, then stopping*)

A moon, a rocket . . . After all, why not? But along with everything else, a thousand swarming, contradictory, real things . . .

ARTHUR:

(*Standing up, waving his hands*)

That's just what I wanted . . . to add . . .

THE OLD MAN:

You can't add to what doesn't exist, and your idea doesn't exist. It's ridiculous, one-sided, simplistic! At best, it's good for amusing schoolchildren, and even then . . .

(*Walking*)

What do children want? They want to be like grown-ups, they want to feel uncertainty, chance; in a word, life.

VICTOR:

(*To Arthur, but for the Old Man's benefit*)

As a matter of fact, Arthur, you must admit that your idea, at least the way you've just presented it, has something incomplete about it, I might even say childish. Besides, please remember that my opinion about it hasn't changed.

(*Timidly approaching the Old Man who is still walking up and down, a prey to the greatest agitation*)

But I wonder if you couldn't consider this idea as an excellent point of departure nevertheless. Certainly it may be inadequate in itself and even erroneous to a certain degree, but all the same, it indicates a step forward, given . . .

ARTHUR:

(*Approaching Victor*)

I'm sorry, but my idea is not as rudimentary as you both seem to think it is.

(*Following the Old Man who is still walking up and down, and himself followed by Victor*)

And if I had had time to talk to you quietly, if we hadn't constantly been interrupted, I would certainly have brought up the problem of method . . . For example, it's perfectly conceivable that the moon . . .

(*He thinks for a moment*)

once the rocket had reached it, would go out before lighting up, and that would require a supplementary stage. Another advantage: when the moon is out and the rockets have disappeared, the spectator and even the inattentive player might be fooled for a moment and think that nothing has happened. So you see, your criticisms are irrelevant. All the more since the rockets' progress doesn't exclude the possibility of a victory by some other means: for instance, the accumulation of points. We therefore have two possibilities . . .

THE OLD MAN:
(*Standing up and facing Arthur*)
Two possibilities!
(*Raising his arms*)
But I need ten, fifteen, fifty!
(*Despairingly*)
Two possibilities, with things the way they are now!
(*Walking*)
Try to use your head. Time's passing, ideas are getting complicated, desires are multiplying, and you expect the players to be satisfied with the regular advance of a rocket toward an invariable goal? No, that's not what they want. And what *do* they want? I don't know. If I knew, I wouldn't be asking you. But in any case, they want something new, something bizarre, something complex!
(*Standing still now and shouting*)
Why don't you turn out the numbers in order, while you're at it!
(*Approaching Arthur and Victor who are bewildered and terrified*)

But use your eyes, damn it! Look around you. Who's
making money today? Property owners? How many property owners are there? Yet every day the racetracks are
jammed, and when I say the racetracks I mean business,
women, war. I mean everything worth loving. I mean
everything people are ready to die for.
(*Thunderously*)
You understand!

(*Arthur and Victor gaping, recoil*)

SCENE SIX

(*A Square. Stage right, a bench. Sitting on it side by side, Annette, Arthur and Victor*)

ANNETTE:
(*Too calm to be reassuring*)
Of course I understand. The time wasn't right for prospectors. Besides, all things considered, this isn't the moment to go into the business. Internal difficulties, the "defection" of the better places, the tentacular development of the pinball arcades have already frightened away a little middle-class girl like me. I'm waiting for better times.

ARTHUR:
(*Standing up*)
Listen, Annette . . .

VICTOR:
(*Standing up*)
Listen, my dear girl, we've done our best, and I wonder who could have done better in our place. I can assure you that your friend Roger wasn't so brilliant either, and for once his natural elegance . . .

ANNETTE:

(*Still sitting, with a slight laugh*)

Couldn't keep him from being thrown out, I know. And I also know that a moment later Sutter . . .

SUTTER:

(*Rushing in stage right*)

So the world still talks about Sutter? Trying to tarnish his reputation all over again. Habit, habit, habit. A set of rusty gears.

(*Turning to Mrs. Duranty who has just entered, panting, stage left*)

There's a ghost for you.

MRS. DURANTY:

I could say the same thing about you, Mr. Sutter.

(*Turning toward Arthur and Victor*)

You've all gotten so friendly now.

(*Gasping*)

Well, what about my machine?

ARTHUR:

Mrs. Duranty, we were just . . . I mean, we were just explaining to Annette that . . .

MRS. DURANTY:

That what? That I have to go on waiting? Oh, I was expecting that one. I was thinking, if I don't see those two soon, it means they have a bad conscience.

VICTOR:

Please, Mrs. Duranty, let's not exaggerate.

MRS. DURANTY:

I'm not the one who's exaggerating. You made me a promise, you're not keeping it, and I still have to gallop around after you, old as I am, sick as I am. And you say I'm exaggerating!

(*Pause*)

I suppose it isn't true? I suppose you didn't tell me I'd have my machine, Mr. Arthur?

(*Imitating Arthur*)

"Credit for you, Mrs. Duranty? Of course. We'll just mention it in the proper quarters and it'll be arranged." You remember, Annette, you were there.

(*Annette laughs*)

And you too, Mr. Victor, you were there too.

VICTOR:

Mrs. Duranty, it seems to me you've known Arthur long enough . . .

ARTHUR:

(*To Victor*)

How could I know?

(*To Mrs. Duranty*)

Believe me, Mrs. Duranty, I would have liked to keep that promise; I made it to you just to be nice, after all. It certainly wasn't a question of duty . . .

ANNETTE:

(*To Sutter, who for a moment now has been walking about, looking around, scratching himself, and laughing*)

Duty? There's an outdated word for you, isn't it, Sutter?

SUTTER:

Oh, words, words . . . traps, all of them.

MRS. DURANTY:

(*To Arthur and Victor*)

In any case, there was a time when you used to talk less, and

(*Laughing nastily*)

do more. Not that I know what you did most of the time, but whenever I needed someone to break my machine, you were always there. . . . And I was foolish enough never to say a thing. . . .

VICTOR:

You've got to keep your dates clear, Mrs. Duranty. I don't see any connection between what happened at the Gayety . . .

SUTTER:

The Gayety! How many memories that brings back.

(*Extending his arms*)

That's where we all met each other. You, Annette—oh, I know, I remember.

(*Annette laughs*)

And you, my friends, so impetuous, so innocent . . .

MRS. DURANTY:

Innocent! That's a good one. They didn't miss a chance to pump me about what was going on at the Corporation. And now that they're there themselves . . .

SUTTER:

And now that they're there themselves, they despise

Sutter, thanks to whom, nevertheless—indirectly, I admit, but all the same . . . they first met Constantine.
(*Pause*)
I must confess I was expecting a gesture—not of gratitude, I don't ask so much as that—but at least of friendship. I've waited, but nothing's come.
(*Sighing*)
Too bad for Sutter!

(*Annette laughs*)

ARTHUR:
(*Who's been controlling himself for some time, approaching Sutter*)
So you think that when you burst into the Corporation like that, in . . . in the very office where the Old Man was talking to us, and right in the middle of a discussion whose results . . .

(*Victor plucks Arthur's sleeve*)

MRS. DURANTY:
Do you hear that, Annette? They see each other at the Corporation all day long!

ANNETTE:
(*Standing up: an outburst*)
Oh yes, they see each other all right! But not at the Corporation. That's really too much!
(*Pointing to Sutter*)
It's been a long time since he's dared stick his nose in there, and

(*Pointing to Arthur and Victor*)

as for these other two, it's even funnier. They've never even set foot in the place.

(*Laughing*)

They were counting on me to get them in. Imagine that! Yes, these gentlemen happened to need shoes at the very moment Roger was coming to see me.

(*To Arthur and Victor*)

Only you didn't do so well with Roger, did you?

(*Sobbing*)

He knows nobody can do anything for anyone! Roger!

(*She runs out stage left*)

ARTHUR:

Annette!

(*He wants to follow her but Victor holds him back by his coattails*)

MRS. DURANTY:

(*Running after Annette*)

Annette, what's the matter? Annie dear, you shouldn't . . . Wait for Mrs. Duranty. Oh, my poor legs.

(*Turning around*)

You can be proud of yourselves, all three of you.

(*She exits, stage left*)

SUTTER:

Women, what a breed!

ARTHUR:

(*Victor still holding him*)

Victor . . . we can't . . . we're not going to let her go away like that without saying anything . . .

(*Victor shrugs his shoulders, lets Arthur go, and starts walking up and down. Arthur turns to Sutter*)

And you? . . . you . . . You couldn't tell her we really did see each other there? It doesn't matter to you if she thinks you . . .

SUTTER:

(*Laughing ruefully*)

Not much. And besides, why should I remind her of that meeting, when you . . .

ARTHUR:

You really didn't expect us to . . .

VICTOR:

(*Who has grown very nervous, to Arthur*)

That's enough nonsense. It's quite natural he wouldn't want to admit his shortcomings just to do you a favor.

(*To Sutter*)

And just between us, I don't think it was such a good idea . . .

SUTTER:

You're wrong. It worked!

(*Pause*)

So you believed that business about Evelyn's being sick; you fell for it too. Well, I happened to be improvising, my friends, improvising. The truth is much more complicated.

(*Pause*)

Enough of this inanity! The situation is serious. Yes, I can

feel the storm coming, and where is it heading? Straight for the Corporation.
(*Sighing*)
Poor Constantine, so many enemies, and in his own house . . .

ARTHUR:
(*Whom the mention of the Corporation has made wildly angry*)
What enemies? If you think it's your business to keep us informed—supposing that you know anything yourself—the least you could do is try . . .

SUTTER:
Don't ask for names. I never give names. It's such a small world—the world of business, of course, not the other one, the real one. Oh, what a life we lead—"in city pent"—what nonsense it all is.

VICTOR:
No one's making you stay in the city. Why don't you go away?

(*Arthur begins walking up and down*)

SUTTER:
I haven't waited for your advice, young man. The die is cast. I'm leaving the Corporation. Too much work and no fun! Constantine will be sorry: I will, too, of course, but I can't help it. Why should I let an opportunity like this pass?
(*Pause*)

(*Victor, too, begins walking. Sutter continues, nevertheless*)

They've offered me—down south, I mean, in the southwest, it doesn't matter—a position as head of an orphan home. I like children, I love the country, and I've accepted it.

(*Pause. He walks and scratches himself*)

You have no idea what a consolation it is for me, knowing that in six weeks I'll be surrounded by little brown or blonde heads looking up at me in the green fields . . .

(*Returning to reality, with an expansive gesture*)

Well, good luck! I leave you to your anthill lives.

(*He exits stage right in a whirlwind of gestures*)

ARTHUR:

(*After a moment's stupefaction*)

But what does he want from us? First the other day at the Old Man's office, on account of him . . . and now again . . .

(*He trembles with rage*)

VICTOR:

Listen, Arthur, Sutter wasn't looking for you, remember that. And if we've got him on our back now with all the rest, including your dear Annette . . .

ARTHUR:

(*Absentmindedly*)

Annette, poor Annette.

VICTOR:

Personally, I have no interest in feeling sorry for Annette. Annette's problems, Sutter's children, the player's mentality, the Corporation's future . . . I'm through with all that.

I'm leaving. My final exams are coming and I'm getting ready for them. Period. That's all. You're free to perfect the rocket now or to invent another moon, but don't count on the old guard any more . . .

(*Victor, his hands in his pockets, begins walking up and down, determined not to listen to any more*)

ARTHUR:

(*Following Victor, stopping, starting again, etc.*)

Really, Victor, you don't mean you want to give everything up just because Sutter . . . who's only a poor fool, after all—you made that quite clear to him yourself, and I'm glad you did.

(*Pause*)

Let's try to take our bearings, please? After all, what's happened? Nothing that isn't rational: we present an idea, it's bad, and it's refused. But we know from experience that all we have to do is offer a good one for it to be . . . immediately accepted. Remember the flippers. Consequently . . .

(*Pause*)

(*Victor is still walking*)

Then, too, the Old Man has nothing against us personally. He said rather disagreeable things to us, of course, but you know him. He always lets himself get carried away by the force of his own words. Besides, you remember how he considered the idea before rejecting it. And in the long run, his criticisms of it were the same as your own. And in a sense you were both right, I admit that.

It was a mistake putting the rocket in the middle, or rather, the mistake was to think that I had to have a middle. Of course there shouldn't be anything there since . . . since the player should be . . . disconcerted.

(*Pause*)

Now how could you disconcert him better than by distracting his attention? In other words, by flashing in each corner of the scoreboard the various visual motifs that would illustrate the different ways of winning.

(*He stops and ponders*)

So once you could invent these motifs . . .

(*He walks and stops again*)

Listen, you could use . . . I don't know . . .

(*Pause, pondering*)

A wrestling match . . .

(*Victor stops and with his hands in his pockets eyes Arthur*)

Or . . .

(*Pause*)

a boat race . . . Or even both together.

(*He ponders and then with a fresh impulse*)

And when one of the wrestlers was pinned or when one of the boats reached the finish . . . then . . .

(*Pause. He ponders*)

Then we'll arrange it so that the winner's harbor lights up . . . or rather . . .

(*He ponders*)

So that they go out and then light up alternately . . . or even . . .

(*He ponders*)
Or even have the harbor light up first and then go out and then the wrestlers the other way around . . . Do you follow me?

VICTOR:
No.

Curtain

PART TWO

SCENE SEVEN

(*A Dancing School. Upstage, somewhat stage left, a phonograph. Also stage left, a couch. Chairs. Mrs. Duranty, whom the spectator sees from the rear, is getting dressed. Victor, not far from her, is gesticulating, a stethoscope in his hand. He is now dressed as a "gentleman."*)

VICTOR:

No, I don't see Arthur any more. I don't go to the Corporation any more either. But why shouldn't I mention Arthur *or* the Corporation if I want to. After all, Arthur was my friend a long time, and it's only natural that once I've passed my examinations and have more time to myself, I should wonder what's happened to him.

MRS. DURANTY:

(*Turning around*)

Arthur! As if he cared about us. Arthur. It's easy to see: I've been sick since September second and he hasn't even bothered . . .

VICTOR:

How do you expect him to find you? You have the fidgets. One day it's a cafe, the next it's a Turkish bath, and now it's a dancing school.

MRS. DURANTY:

But you, Mr. Victor, even though you're so busy, you seem able to . . .

VICTOR:

I'm sorry, Mrs. Duranty, but you came to look for me yourself. Of course, when it's a question of getting yourself taken care of, of being looked after at state expense . . .

MRS. DURANTY:

Well, of course. If *I* could find you, Mr. Victor, then Arthur could have too. Only that's just it. He doesn't care about his old friends any more. What interests him is the Corporation. And that Corporation of his is really taking a beating.

VICTOR:

Please don't start that again I beg you. Obviously the Corporation's problems amuse you: no more machines in public places. So you got your revenge at last.

MRS. DURANTY:

I wish I did, but what about the pinball arcades? What are you going to do about that? I'm sure I don't know. Imagine, I even have one

(*Pointing stage right*)

out there, just across the street, right under my nose, and I have to put up with it.

VICTOR:

I know, I know.

MRS. DURANTY:

I tell you, it's no pleasure either. Right in the middle of a lesson they run out on me to have a game and then they come back out of breath and red all over . . . Pouah!

(*Pause*)

And when I think of all that money going straight into the Corporation's pockets . . .

VICTOR:

Not for long. You can reassure yourself on that score. The pinball arcades are going to be nationalized soon. And let me tell you personally, I won't be sorry about that . . . The only thing that worries me, if you'll forgive my saying so, is to think that Arthur, fool that he is, doesn't realize how serious the situation is. I know him. If he doesn't have someone reasonable around, he'll go on wasting his time and ranting on and on . . .

MRS. DURANTY:

Wasting his time? As if he ever did anything else. And you, Mr. Victor, if you start seeing him again, you'll be wasting your time, too.

VICTOR:

(*Putting away his instruments*)

While with you, of course, I never . . . Well, good-bye, Mrs. Duranty. You're as strong as an ox and you don't need me any more.

(*He puts his instruments in his little bag, puts on his coat and is about to exit stage right*)

MRS. DURANTY:

(Running after him)

Mr. Victor, you're not going to abandon me? What's going to become of me, all alone? And what about the Urodonal, with my bronchitis? . . . They don't go together. What about . . .

VICTOR:

Oh yes, yes they do. And I'll come by again, don't you worry.

(Exit)

MRS. DURANTY:

(Returning stage center)

What you don't have to put up with when you need people!

(Long pause while Mrs. Duranty finishes dressing)

(Enter stage right Mr. Roger and the Old Man, bundled into an overcoat that is too big for him)

(Throwing up her hands)

Mr. Roger! Imagine!

THE OLD MAN:

You know each other?

MR. ROGER:

(Embarrassed and aloof)

Yes, this lady used to run a cafe where I went sometimes.

THE OLD MAN:

And you didn't even want to come in here. That's just like you, Roger. Typical.

(*Pause*)

I'm very pleased, Mrs. . . .

MRS. DURANTY:

(*Vaguely curtseying*)

. . . Mrs. Duranty, professor of the dance, a poor woman who asks your indulgence because tonight she has only one girl . . . Bronchitis, of course, a winter like this.

MR. ROGER:

We didn't come here to dance.

MRS. DURANTY:

You didn't come to . . .

THE OLD MAN:

(*Looking around the stage*)

Well, you have a waxed floor, a phonograph, a little sofa, everything you need. Except, of course, a pinball machine.

MRS. DURANTY:

But, sir, I'm not the only one. No one has them any more. It's not allowed. You know that.

THE OLD MAN:

(*In the tone of the political demagogue on an electoral tour, which he keeps until the end of the scene*)

And you accept this prohibition? You're being deprived of your livelihood without protest, not a peep? Not one complaint . . .

MRS. DURANTY:

Oh, you know. I'm used to it. It's been a long time since I've had a machine. . . . The Corporation took mine back to fix it for me, or so they said, and that was the end of that. Never seen nor heard of again . . .

(*Turning toward Mr. Roger*)

Mr. Roger can tell you about it . . .

(*Mr. Roger signals to Mrs. Duranty to keep quiet*)

THE OLD MAN:

(*To Mr. Roger*)

What? You knew this lady was without her machine and didn't tell me? Even stupider than I thought.

MR. ROGER:

Listen, Mr. Constantine . . .

MRS. DURANTY:

Mr. Constantine! You're Mr. Constantine! And here I was . . . and about the Corporation . . .

THE OLD MAN:

Don't apologize. You're really doing us a favor. It's never too late to put our finger on the errors we've committed —or let others commit . . .

(*Serious*)

Errors without which, perhaps, we wouldn't be where we are today.

MRS. DURANTY:

Then it's true, isn't it, Mr. Constantine . . . You have your problems, too.

THE OLD MAN:

Problems which we have deserved, dear lady.

(*He takes off his overcoat, which Mrs. Duranty eagerly takes from his hands, and sits down on the couch*)

For we're guilty, yes, guilty, both of us. You of not having

trusted me, of not having come to see me personally, as
an ally, as a friend, and I of not always having maintained
my contacts with people I refuse to call my customers
because they are my associates.

(*After a pause*)

After all . . .

(*Pause*)

Dear lady, our interests coincide, for actually who manu-
factures the machine? I do. Who takes care of it? You do.
And here we are, both of us at grips with the same enemy,
the State, a licensed bandit which does not hesitate to
appropriate the fruits of our labor.

(*Pause*)

What weapons have we against it? One alone: to join
hands, you and I.

MRS. DURANTY:

(*A "poor little thing," standing before the Old Man*)

You and I . . .

THE OLD MAN:

Exactly.

(*To Mr. Roger, who obviously would like to be somewhere else*)

Well, what are you waiting for? Your head's always buried
somewhere. Give me the list.

(*Mr. Roger takes out of his pocket a large sheet of paper
which the Old Man snatches out of his hands to hand to
Mrs. Duranty*)

Read that, dear lady.

Mrs. Duranty:

(*After having read it*)

Oh, a petition . . . My goodness, you have a lot of names there.

The Old Man:

And I'll have one more when you sign yours, Mrs. . . .

(*Trying to remember the name*)

Duranty.

Mrs. Duranty:

You want me to sign it? But since my machine already . . . before . . . it's not the State that . . .

The Old Man:

(*Standing up*)

Well then, after all I've said, you still consider yourself banished from the community of my associate concession-aires? Now look here, I've come to see you. You've informed me of your situation, and the one thing that still keeps me from helping you is precisely the State's decision. Therefore, what still remains for you to do? Sign. Integrate yourself with this righteous throng. In other words, associate your name with this collective protest which will intimidate the authorities and force them to retreat. We will not suffer this injustice any longer. You must recover possession of your rights, like everyone else.

Mr. Roger:

(*Impatiently*)

Sign here.

(*He indicates a place on the sheet*)

MRS. DURANTY:

Sign, sign. That's all very well, Mr. Roger, but once I'm down there with all those others, who am I? You'll forget about me . . . with my usual luck . . .

THE OLD MAN:

Come now, this is one occasion when fortune is smiling on you. . . . Think it over. All the rest are in the same situation, the common situation, whereas you, you are the rare case, the particular case. The first chance I have to glance at this list, your name will leap to my eyes: Mrs. Duranty, the concessionaire prematurely injured, and you'll be automatically included among those first served.

MRS. DURANTY:

Yes, you, you know, but the others . . .

THE OLD MAN:

They'll know too.

(*Pause*)

What we'll do is just underline your name right here and now.

MRS. DURANTY:

But, Mr. Constantine, if you put it like that, so prominently, suppose the paper falls into the hands of . . . of the people who run the pinball arcades . . . You have to be careful with those Armenians . . . Oh, they wouldn't do anything to *you*, of course. They wouldn't dare. But I'm just a poor old woman . . .

MR. ROGER:

(*Impatiently*)

The pinball arcades! If you think the pinball arcades are going to bother . . .

THE OLD MAN:

And why wouldn't they bother about Mrs. Duranty? Can't you open your mouth without saying some nonsense or other? I suppose Mrs. Duranty doesn't count?

(*Pause*)

You're entirely justified, dear lady, in raising that objection. It proves you know what you're talking about. But you're making one little mistake, nevertheless. You're forgetting how easily intimidated people of that sort are. A name underlined means an important person and therefore a dangerous person, someone it would be to their advantage to conciliate—at any cost.

(*Smiling*)

If I know you, you'll make a little pin money out of this . . .

MRS. DURANTY:

(*Smiling, a little senile*)

Well then . . .

(*She signs*)

(*Enter Annette stage left, her hair up, wearing a short, between-seasons coat. She sees Mr. Roger at once and stops*)

Annette dear, come quick. Imagine what's happened to us! This gentleman . . .

(*She points to the Old Man*)

Guess who he is. Mr. Constantine! Yes, in person.

ANNETTE:

Mr. Constantine, I'm delighted. But he hasn't come alone.
Hello, Roger.
(*Laughing*)
Still shipshape?

(*Mr. Roger, who despite everything, had hoped not to be
seen, stammers*)

THE OLD MAN:

(*Obviously intrigued by Annette, to Mr. Roger*)
Ah, so you know this lady, too. And I didn't know anything about it. Better and better. Quite a private life.

MR. ROGER:

Constantine, I'd have been happy to introduce you to my
friend Annie, I've always meant to, but . . .

THE OLD MAN:

But what?

MR. ROGER:

But . . . she's rather shy. At least, she used to be. And
perhaps she wouldn't have dared . . .

THE OLD MAN:

What? A girl as ravishing as that, shy?
(*To Annette*)
Honestly, Miss, are you . . .

ANNETTE:

(*Laughing*)
No, I wasn't afraid to be exposed to your eyes. Only what
Roger didn't tell you is that not only did he want to intro-

duce me to you, he had a special plan which rather did intimidate me, I must admit.

(*A little nasally, staring Mr. Roger down*)

He wanted me to work as a prospector for the Corporation.

(*Mr. Roger, bewildered, moves as far away as possible*)

MRS. DURANTY:

No, you're geting mixed up, Annie dear. That was Mr. Sutter.

THE OLD MAN:

(*Dumbfounded*)

Sutter? Sutter used to come here?

MRS. DURANTY:

(*Beating a retreat*)

Oh, you know, Mr. Constantine. It's just a name. It might have been someone else. . . . You know how it is in cafes, you see so many people . . .

THE OLD MAN:

Let's forget about it.

(*Pause, then to Mr. Roger*)

So for once in your life you had a good idea and you decided to keep it shut up in that little brain of yours.

(*To Annette*)

Of course, you could have come to work for us. It was even in the cards.

(*Pause*)

How unfortunate. Good God, what a mistake!

(*Pause*)

But come now, we're not going to let a little thing like that go by without . . .

MR. ROGER:

(*No longer able to contain himself*)

I'm sorry, Constantine, but even admitting her cooperation might have been valuable to us once, it seems to me that at present . . .

(*Annette laughs slightly*)

THE OLD MAN:

Now it's defeatism!

MRS. DURANTY:

I don't understand, Mr. Roger. Just a minute ago you made me sign and now . . .

(*To the Old Man*)

Everything's going to be all right, isn't it, Mr. Constantine? Aren't I going to have my machine?

THE OLD MAN:

Of course you are. But we have to have help. And where can we find it? Where save from young, dynamic, enthusiastic workers.

(*To Annette*)

Like you, my dear.

MRS. DURANTY:

Tell me, Mr. Constantine, when you come down to it, it *was* just a poor old woman who signed your petition for you, after all?

(*The Old Man raises his arms over his head, threatening. Mrs. Duranty shrinks back*)

ANNETTE:

(Nastily)

Calm yourself, Mrs. Duranty. I have no desire to come between you and the Corporation. Besides, I don't see what a simple manicurist . . .

MRS. DURANTY:

Now you're not going to blame me for having advised you to become a manicurist. . . . Remember, when you were seeing Arthur . . .

THE OLD MAN:

A manicurist? You're a manicurist? What a splendid position. So intimate, and at the same time so public . . .

(Lyrically)

When you hold someone's hands, you hold him, so to speak, in your power. A word, a pressure, and he obeys.

(He takes Annette's hand, who snatches it away from him at once)

My dear, may I speak to you with an open heart?

ANNETTE:

Please do, dear Mr. Constantine.

THE OLD MAN:

(Sitting down)

Here's the situation. We have important, even powerful enemies, and they take advantage of our slightest hesitation, our slightest error, to spy on us, to compromise us, to ruin us. . . . Today our most immediate task is to thwart their maneuvers. In other words, to find someone who can

infiltrate into the circles where those manuevers are being
devised.
(*Standing up*)
Yes, someone who knows how to use influence, encourage
one decision, deter another.
(*Approaching Annette, whose hand he tries to take again*)
Now, who could do such a thing better, more effectively
and more discreetly, too, than a manicurist? . . .

ANNETTE:
(*Retreating*)
And the manicurist spy—would be me?
(*She laughs*)

THE OLD MAN:
(*Somewhat taken aback*)
Why not?
(*To Mr. Roger, who has sat down and is swinging his leg*)
You, of course, have nothing to say? Perhaps you don't
agree?

MR. ROGER:
(*Distressed at having to take part*)
Of course, Constantine, I . . . quite agree . . .

ANNETTE:
(*Letting herself go*)
There we are. Everybody understands everybody else and
everyone agrees. But maybe I have something to say, too.
I think you ought to know that what happens to a Corporation on the way down interests me about as much as
what happens on the moon. Good-bye, gentlemen.

(*She exits quickly, stage right*)

THE OLD MAN:

(*Holding out his arms*)

Roger, what's the matter with her? Do something. Run after her and bring her back. Bring her back!

(*Mr. Roger, hesitating briefly, obeys, and exits stage right. Mrs. Duranty, alarmed by the turn events have taken, fusses around the Old Man, who is quite beside himself, and makes him sit down.*)

MRS. DURANTY:

Don't get so upset, Mr. Constantine. You must give them time enough to talk to each other . . .

(*Leaning toward the Old Man, whose face she almost touches*)

These things can always be arranged.

SCENE EIGHT

(*A Square. No one sitting on the bench. Arthur, even more nervous than in Part One, is standing stage center. Stage left, Victor. Stage right, Annette.*)

ARTHUR:
(*Turning toward Victor*)
But after all, Victor, what makes you think the Old Man's petition is so certain to fail? In any case, the mere fact that at his age and in his position, he's trying such a thing proves his vitality and the Corporation's too. And above all, don't tell me I'm getting overwrought. I happen to have grown very level-headed. Yes, during all these months when you haven't deigned to see me . . .
(*Turning to Annette*)
You either, Annette, you never came . . .
(*Turning again toward Victor, who is obviously impatient with him*)
During all these months I haven't made a move. First of all, I admit it, because without you I didn't have the energy, the freedom, I mean the freedom of mind I needed to go back there. But also because I gradually

realized that all our mistakes resulted, in part at least, from our hastiness or, let's say, from my own anyway. But that's not a reason to discourage me altogether, especially when, as I told you, I've thought up some ideas which without being absolutely conclusive are nevertheless beginning to get organized, to take shape; and it's still less a reason to treat Annette like a liar when, after all, you haven't seen *her* for a long time either.

(*Very aggressive*)

Because you *have* treated her like a liar, you know, just because she told us that things weren't so desperate after all.

ANNETTE:

And I have good reasons for thinking so. Because don't forget, dear Victor, your information is secondhand . . .

(*Laughing*)

The first hand being Mrs. Duranty, while I've lived through the events *in person*.

VICTOR:

Yes, as far as Mrs. Duranty goes, I agree with you. But let me ask you one very simple question, dear Annette. If the Old Man's situation seems so promising to you, why did you refuse his proposition?

ARTHUR:

Annette is absolutely free to prefer being a manicurist to some other job. After all, as she's just told you, being a manicurist doesn't lack . . .

VICTOR:

(*Imitating Annette*)

"Psychological interest," "intimacy with the customer." I know . . .

ARTHUR:

(*To Victor*)

That isn't the question.

(*Turning to Annette*)

To tell the truth, Annette, there really is something . . . that's bothering me a little. I don't know how to explain it to you.

(*Pause*)

If you've rejected the offers they've made you it seems to me rather difficult, I don't say impossible, but difficult, that in the future you should find if not the opportunity, at least the possibility . . .

ANNETTE:

Of talking to him about you? Now just a minute. I didn't say *no* straight off and stupid like a little girl. I—distilled my refusal.

(*Laughing*)

Don't worry, they'll come back running. And when they do I'll know what to say next: "You're renewing your formula? Fine. But renew your models too." You can see the transition . . .

(*Spinning around*)

Oh yes, Annette's faithful enough, despite her whims.

ARTHUR:

Annette . . .

ANNETTE:

Besides, I've already dropped hints. I've hinted at getting rid of the flippers, and the idea of the moon, too.

(*Victor, who in his annoyance has moved away a little, sneers*)

ARTHUR:

(*Moved*)
The moon? Oh, you talked about the moon . . .
(*Suddenly frightened*)
But maybe you shouldn't have. Remember . . .

VICTOR:

(*Laughing nastily*)
What're you talking about, Annette? The rocket and the moon was your mutual masterpiece, the single child of those two great minds.

ANNETTE:

Why shouldn't I have talked about the moon? Just because the idea didn't happen to please that old Constantine one day? He's forgotten it ages ago, that poor moon. At the most, the word only vaguely reminds him . . .
(*To Arthur*)
of your existence . . .
(*To Victor*)
or of our existence, if you prefer.

ARTHUR:

But, Annette, you . . . do you honestly think we ought to . . . that right now . . .

ANNETTE:

(*Very businesslike*)
No, not right now. You have to leave me time to work and then at the right moment . . .

(*Enter stage right Sutter, somewhat aged and very ragged and wretched looking. He's carrying a bundle of tracts under one arm, one or two falling as he walks. Arthur is evidently dumbfounded. Victor, however, controls himself*)

SUTTER:

Well, this *is* a conspiracy! Glad to see you, all three of you. It's been a long time. Ah, youth . . . youth passes . . .
(*Pause*)
Have you heard the latest? Poor Constantine, in the soup, along with the whole Corporation!

ANNETTE:

And where did you get your pretty news, Sutter? Rumors? Gossip? People make mistakes sometimes, and in any case, my news is far from being so
(*Laughing*)
alarming.

VICTOR:

(*To Annette*)
Well, personally, I'm afraid he's right.

(*To no one in particular*)
And I don't see any reason why you should all . . .

ARTHUR:

(*To Sutter*)
Whatever's happened, I'm surprised you're still interested
in matters you . . . Well, what about your plans . . .

ANNETTE:

(*Who a moment before had picked up one of the tracts
Sutter dropped and who has had a chance to read it*)
Ah, so you've come to this!
(*Handing tracts to Arthur and even to Victor who ignores
her*)
Take a look at that, my friends.

ARTHUR:

(*After having read the tract*)
That's . . . that's really too much . . .
(*To Sutter*)
Really, after all that Mr. Constantine has done for you,
or at least all that you tried to make him to do for you,
you . . . you dare to spread propaganda like this? I won't
even call it low, since it's really . . .
(*Pause*)
Are they paying you a lot to do this?

(*Victor, during Arthur's speech, has been trying to take the
tract from him, but Arthur resists. Victor, tired of struggling,
approaches Suttter and takes a tract out of the bundle that
he is still carrying under his arm, after which he reads it*

at stage right, one foot on the bench, still following the conversation, of course)

SUTTER:

Don't condemn me too quickly, young men. You don't know. He's guilty too. Our past, our youth, reading together around the campfire, he's forgotten it all, rubbed it all out at one stroke. What can I do? Forgive him? Perhaps. But meanwhile I have to live, eat, dress myself. It's easy to say you can retreat to the desert . . .

ANNETTE:

Splendid. Continue on your glorious path.

(*Laughing*)

And I know one person who will be quite interested in your new activities when I inform him of them.

SUTTER:

The little lackey, of course?

ANNETTE:

No, the master himself.

(*Laughing*)

Oh, not that I think you, or rather your employers, represent a serious danger for Constantine, but I'd like him to know the regrettable evolution of his childhood friend. . . . Bye-bye, Sutter. I'm expected . . .

(*Sententiously*)

at the Corporation.

(*She holds out her hand to Arthur*)

ARTHUR:

Annette . . . you're not going to leave now, when we

haven't . . . we have to . . . if we . . . you understand . . .

ANNETTE:

(*Going off, more casual than ever*)

Don't worry. I'll take care of everything and I'll call you when we need you.

(*She exits stage left*)

SUTTER:

Poor little fool. As if Constantine didn't know Sutter.

ARTHUR:

He knows Sutter so well you probably felt it wasn't necessary to explain anything to him . . .

SUTTER:

(*His arms outstretched*)

But of course I tried to have an explanation. Why only the other day I rushed in to see him, at closing time. Only Roger wouldn't let me in.

(*Pause*)

Yes, there was Sutter standing at Constantine's door, his collar up under the driving rain. Now I've seen everything.

(*Walking up and down*)

Don't tell me he wasn't there. I heard them whispering, both of them. And besides . . . and besides . . .

(*Shouting*)

I know he's sick.

ARTHUR:

(*Unable to endure it any longer and advancing toward Sutter*)

Sick! But Annette saw him . . . the day before yesterday,
so . . .

(*Sutter eyes Arthur threateningly. Victor, concerned, runs
up to distract him*)

VICTOR:
(*To Arthur whom he separates from Sutter*)
What does it matter what Annette saw?
(*To Sutter, almost politely*)
What's the matter with him, with the Old Man? You can
tell me. I'm a doctor.

SCENE NINE

(*Darkness. Spotlights on Arthur and Victor, the latter carry-ing a little black bag. They take several steps to stage left and then stop.*)

VICTOR:

If they let us come in together, fine. Otherwise I'll arrange it so that during the consultation I can sound out the terrain and if it's possible, even mention you right off.
(*Pause*)
The important thing is to see him, isn't it? Now, since Mrs. Duranty's told him I'm coming . . .

ARTHUR:

She promised she would, but . . .

VICTOR:

No buts. Mrs. Duranty needs me and since the Old Man needs her too . . .

ARTHUR:

Don't get angry, Victor. I know you're doing everything you can and I'm . . . very grateful to you for it. But I can't help worrying a little. We decided all this so quickly . . .

VICTOR:

We didn't have any choice. We have to act now or never. Still, I grant you what we're doing is rather unlikely, but I couldn't stand it any more, I couldn't stand your nagging night and day about Annette's influence, Annette's kindness, Annette's position at the Corporation . . .

(*Darkness. When the lights come up we are in the Old Man's room. Stage left, a bed. In the bed, lying facing the audience, the Old Man. To his left, kneeling and holding his hand, Mr. Roger, evidently helpless and distressed. To his right, sitting on a chair and "doing" his other hand, Annette, elegant and remorseful.*)

THE OLD MAN:

(*Starting abruptly out of his nap, forcing Annette to let go of his hand*)

It's our prices that are ruining us! If the buyer can't keep up with us any more, it's up to us to drop ballast. The "status quo?" Failure, cooperatives, the end of everything.

(*Shouting to Mr. Roger*)

Is that what you want?

MR. ROGER:

No, Mr. Constantine. I'm . . . quite in agreement with you. . . . We'll have to lower our prices . . . but maybe this isn't the right moment to . . . considering . . . our difficulties . . .

ANNETTE:

(*Almost laughing*)

Don't pay any attention to him, Mr. Constantine. I know him. He's afraid lowering prices will mean neglecting quality, and he thinks quality . . .

(*To Roger*)

You can't always be worrying about ideals in this world. It's too exhausting and in the long run, it's dangerous too.

THE OLD MAN:

The voice of reason!

(*Attempting to caress Annette, who vaguely permits him to do so*)

So fragile and yet so businesslike!

(*Laughing*)

Wonderful little creature.

(*Shouting*)

Quality! But it's quantity that counts, God damn it! Why not sell cheap machines as long as they look good? They break down quicker? Big deal! Mechanism? Gears? That can all be replaced!

(*Pause*)

The concessionaires? They'll get what's coming to them, all of it! New machines, new customers. You've got to work on the eyes—the power of display, increasing the demand in order to increase the supply . . .

(*He caresses Annette*)

as some American once said, I believe.

MR. ROGER:

Yes, I think it was.

(*Annette laughs*)

THE OLD MAN:

(*With a deep sigh*)

He thinks it was.

MR. ROGER:

(*Standing up, with apparent energy*)

Excuse me, but I still have one more objection. . . . If the machines break down, there'll be . . . expenses that won't be covered perhaps . . .

(*He sits down on a chair near the bed*)

ANNETTE:

(*To Mr. Roger*)

So it bothers you when they change the machines from time to time? You think they're irreplaceable?

THE OLD MAN:

There's your comeuppance, Roger. She's not easy to get around, is she?

(*He laughs and caresses Annette, who squirms away from him*)

But wait a minute, I haven't said my last word yet.

(*Shouting*)

Increasing the number of machines is all right, but increasing the number of models is even better.

(*He laughs*)

Of course, that makes expenses, big expenses, but that's the way we have to do it.

(*Shouting and sitting up in his bed*)

Or else . . . or else it's nothing but inchworm progress!

(*Turning to Mr. Roger*)

Isn't that right?

(*He falls back on his pillow*)

MR. ROGER:

(*Bustling about the Old Man*)

Yes, you're right, Mr. Constantine, of course . . .

(*Looking for something say*)

We have to increase the number of models, too.

ANNETTE:

(*Bored with a mauling constantly accompanied by conversations with Mr. Roger*)

Forgive me, Mr. Constantine, if I'm speaking over and above my station, but I don't see why you need so many different models.

(*She stands up and speaks very loudly to Mr. Roger*)

You play with the machine that's there. What's the use of looking for new distractions? After all, it's always the same, that's obvious right away. What you need is to have a lot of machines, as many as you can have. Big machines, little machines, machines that work, machines that don't: what's the difference?

THE OLD MAN:

(*Seriously hampered by senility, to Mr. Roger*)

Ah, she's angry with you. What did you do to her?

(*Annette laughs*)

And to think we were so stupid as to cut down the number of models of our own accord!

(*Sitting up*)

Nevertheless, there used to be no lack of ideas. Plenty of propositions. They've been bringing us ideas we should have examined, considered, maybe rejected, but maybe,

after thinking them over—not blindly . . . even from a bad
idea you can sometimes extract . . .
(*Pause*)
Of course, there are inventors . . . but even so, we've got
time. We could make some arrangements and . . . maybe
set a percentage.
(*To Mr. Roger, collapsing on his pillow*)
Go get me the files.
(*To Annette*)
Don't stand over there, dear. Here. You'll be more com-
fortable.
(*He forces Annette to sit down on the bed*)
We'll look all this over together. And I'm sure you'll have
a few little suggestions to make, too.
(*He laughs, then shouting to Mr. Roger off-stage*)
Hurry up! Annette's going to work with us.
(*Pause*)
I guess I'm pretty lucky. You don't find little girls by the
barrel who come of their own accord to do a poor sick
man's hands and who like to stick their nose into his work
into the bargain.
(*He laughs obscenely*)

(*Mr. Roger returns in silence and hands the Old Man the
files*)

(*Choosing a file at random*)
This one, for instance. The left alley at the same time as
the right. At the same time! Why bother with a left and
a right if they're doing the same thing? A one-eyed man

must have thought that one up! Nonsense! And we paid money for that?

(*Pause*)

Oh, this one. Luckily, we refused it: the balls go into holes and stay there. What else? No bottom flippers, nothing at all, huh? Not even a last chance, *in extremis*? And we even bothered to look at it . . .

(*Pause*)

And yet we refused, yes refused, "the bull and the tomato." What did you all have against the bull anyway, you and the rest?

MR. ROGER:

But I never said . . .

THE OLD MAN:

Naturally.

(*Annette laughs*)

Never a word, never any advice. But if you don't know anything, why don't you say so, and I'll hire another secretary, other secretaries, and *they'll* know, *they'll* talk it over, *they'll* always be ready.

(*Pause*)

You can't work by yourself all the time, or you're lost. What do I know about the machine? Nothing. I'm as lost as anyone else . . . To know about the machine you have to talk, talk . . .

(*A bell rings*)

Tell them to come in, it doesn't matter who, we'll talk.

Anyone except the doctor. No doctors!
(*Exit Mr. Roger*)

ANNETTE:
(*Who has stood up, in the calm tone of the well-mannered servant*)
I'll leave you now, Mr. Constantine.

THE OLD MAN:
(*Forcing Annette to sit down again*)
No, my pet. You're not in the way. You're never in the way. I've no secrets from you, and you know it.
(*Laughing*)
Are you so shy of strangers? After all, we're getting to know each other . . .

VICTOR:
(*Off-stage*)
Arthur, Arthur!

(*Annette gives a start, but doesn't move. Enter stage right Arthur, preceded by Mr. Roger. Annette still doesn't move. Arthur, seeing Annette, remains transfixed for a moment, then gets hold of himself as well as he can*)

THE OLD MAN:
(*To Arthur*)
Oh, it's you. Well, I'm glad. Now we can talk a little.
(*To Annette*)
The boy you see in front of you now conceived the "Tilt."

ARTHUR:
Ah, you remember.

THE OLD MAN:

I should say so. A remarkable idea, the "Tilt."

ARTHUR:

(*As if he were taking a header, still staring at Annette who doesn't budge*)

Yes, the first time I came about the "Tilt," but afterwards we brought you other ideas. I say "we" because there were two of us then, and that's why I . . . I'm a little surprised that today

(*Indicating Mr. Roger, who has sat down again*)

he didn't let my friend in . . .

(*Pause*)

Besides, one of our ideas *did* interest you, since . . . getting rid of the flippers, that was us . . .

THE OLD MAN:

Look at these young people, Roger. They get an idea, and then what do you think? They get another. Inexhaustible!

ARTHUR:

(*Aggressive, staring at Annette*)

Obviously our last idea, I mean the last one we brought you, wasn't so good.

THE OLD MAN:

(*To Mr. Roger*)

You see. They can even disapprove of their own ideas. Self-criticism, isn't that what it's called?

(*To Arthur*)

And why wasn't it a good idea? Tell us that.

(*Pause*)

(*Arthur remains silent*)

ANNETTE:

(*Bursts out laughing, to Arthur*)
Don't make such a face. Are you afraid about the rocket?
But I'm going to tell Mr. Constantine about the rocket
and about the moon, too.
(*To the Old Man*)
Maybe you remember. He brought you an idea about a
rocket and the moon and now he's ashamed of it, as he
should be, but I ought to say that I was somewhat respon-
sible . . .

THE OLD MAN:

(*To Mr. Roger*)
Look, look how she goes at it. It's a pleasure to watch her.
Why, we've got a little team building up here. It makes
me feel younger just watching them.
(*He seizes Annette around the waist. She frees herself
but remains sitting on the bed*)

ANNETTE:

(*To Arthur*)
Go on, talk. I suppose if you came here on *your own* today
to see Mr. Constantine, it was because you had an idea
to tell him about.
(*Laughing*)
An idea of your own.

THE OLD MAN:

(*Laughing*)
She's in a hurry. Don't worry, dear. He'll unpack his wares.

All right, my boy. On the track.

ARTHUR:

(*Wild-eyed and very fast*)

All right, yes. I've worked out a whole machine. I've even given it a name: "On Earth As It Is In Heaven." A very simple symbol that sums it all up. On the scoreboard, skaters move forward and airplanes crash.

THE OLD MAN:

(*To Mr. Roger, who is increasingly distressed and despondent*)

You see, Roger, skaters! That's almost what we said before. Remember the three sisters! I think we're on the right track.

ARTHUR:

(*His teeth clenched, faster and faster*)

I didn't stop there, of course. Because I'm moving in your direction, or at least the direction you pointed out to me a long time ago. Yes, you once said to me . . .

(*He stares at Annette*)

that there had to be several ways of winning, or rather not several, thousands. In my machine you can win either by score, by points, by bonus, by the numbers put out, by the numbers lit up, by the holes in a straight line, by the holes in a V, and even by the top hole, not to mention the alleys.

THE OLD MAN:

(*Laughs obscenely*)

Ah, the alleys. It's because they're so narrow.

(*He caresses Annette*)

ARTHUR:

(*Icily*)

That's just it, the alleys.

(*Pause*)

Now I'm coming to my main idea: we've always over-estimated the importance of the flippers.

THE OLD MAN:

(*Gradually seized by the euphoria of the total paralytic*)

I agree with you a hundred percent. You see, Roger, the same thing as for the three sisters. Just one flipper for all three cuties.

ARTHUR:

That's right. You see, up to now, we've always thought you had to work the flipper to get into an alley and light it up. That's wrong . . . because in the other alleys there are arrows that light up only when the ball rolls over them . . . and . . . not always then, so we have to learn how to resist the temptation of the flippers. The ball rolls and you let it roll and you can't tell . . .

THE OLD MAN:

You can't tell! You've really got some good ones. In this business you have to be ready for anything!

(*He caresses Annette once more but she squirms impatiently away from him.*)

ARTHUR:

(*Just as impatient as Annette*)

I can see we're going to have trouble understanding each

other, and under these conditions perhaps I'd better leave, for my principle remains unchanged. The alleys are only one example among many others, and if my game doesn't interest you . . .

THE OLD MAN:

Don't get so excited, young man. You don't want me to talk back, is that it? What we need is a challenge. Nothing good, nothing important, ever comes out of a monologue.

ARTHUR:

All right. What I consider the essential point finally is in the holes. . . . It's in the holes that we have every imaginable possibility. You have to consider the holes from the game's beginning to its end as an opportunity of winning and a danger of losing. You have to be afraid of them, and at the same time, to hope for them. You aim for them and if you miss them, maybe that's lucky. You aim for them and you make them, and maybe that's lucky, too. You can't tell.

(*Pause*)

But the luckiest of all, the only thing there's no doubt about, is what I call in English, since English is the pinball language, the "return ball." Why do I call it that? Because the ball that falls into that hole returns to the player underneath the board by an underground passageway and so becomes a free ball, a happy ball.

THE OLD MAN:

Yes, there's nothing like beginning all over again.

(*He giggles and makes another pass at Annette, who this time stands up*)

ARTHUR:

(*Aggressively*)

But look out! There's not a hole on the board that you can call *a priori* the "return ball." Sometimes it's one, sometimes another, and sometimes there isn't any return ball at all. Because if you knew ahead of time what the chances were, then it would just be ordinary pleasure, drudgery . . . all over again.

THE OLD MAN:

(*Guffawing*)

Oh, those damn balls! What flirts they are! They're not through fooling everyone they know. They disappear into their hole and you think they're gone, buried, and then, hop! there they are, ready to start all over again and they run and they jump and they go like the wind, for the cuties have caught their breath in the meantime. Oh, they're tricky!

ARTHUR:

(*Drunk with rage*)

Of course, the "return ball," supposing that it exists, is only worth one ball out of every five. Naturally, you can't make the game last forever.

THE OLD MAN:

But what does it matter if the game is longer? We make it cost more and then . . . everybody'll be satisfied.

(*Guffawing continuously until the end of the scene*)

Everyone knows that the longer the better, or rather, excuse me, the more you get out of it. If it costs ten francs now, then we'll make it cost fifty. The important thing is that a good, fat coin goes into the slot. The slot's too small? That doesn't matter. We'll widen it. Fifty francs and the three little sisters light up!

(*Pause. Panting*)

We all have coins like that in our pockets, so let's use them . . . let's use them . . .

(*The Old Man crawls out of his bed to try to grab Annette. He is wearing a long white nightshirt. Annette recoils, terrified. The manicure instruments fall to the floor. Arthur and Mr. Roger stand transfixed*)

(*Panting and falling back on his bed*)
Roger!

(*Mr. Roger rushes forward, catching the Old Man, dying, in his arms*)

SCENE TEN

(*A Square. Annette and Mr. Roger sitting on a bench, stage right. Mr. Roger, very pale, has laid a cane down nearby. He is no longer wearing his usual flower in his buttonhole, but a black ribbon. Besides, he is wearing an enormous bandage and a slipper on one foot. Annette, too, is very pale.*)

ANNETTE:

(*Standing up*)

Now look, a man like Sutter has only one desire in the whole world. He wants to betray his master, whoever he is. And even if he thinks the Corporation hasn't the slightest chance of surviving, he'd be only too happy to do counter-espionage work. I'm not saying he'd sell his secrets to anyone who came along, but to me he will. I know how to talk to him, and besides, he's afraid of me.

MR. ROGER:

(*Calmly, in a very sad tone of voice which he uses until the end of the scene*)

I don't think we can really rely on Sutter, Annie.

ANNETTE:

(*Exasperated*)

Well then, think of something else . . .

MR. ROGER:

What? I can't think of anything. And I . . . and I'm too tired, Annie.

ANNETTE:

(*Gloomily*)

I know, your leg.

(*A prey to her demon again*)

But I'm bored with always hearing you complain about your leg. Whose fault was it, after all? What earthly reason was there for carrying those piles of files down a dark stairway . . . and why *those* files into the bargain! So you've been spending your evenings worrying about other people's ideas again?

MR. ROGER:

Yes, I happen to have been rereading the plans that have been submitted to Mr. Constantine.

ANNETTE:

But, my poor friend, that's absolutely morbid, and quite useless besides. And even if you had ever been interested in that poor machine . . . But you never cared about it and not only it, but about those who loved it, and those who were working on it . . . including Sutter. Because Sutter loved it too, you know. When I think that the only reason you ever got into the Corporation was because . . .

(*She stops, choked by rage*)

MR. ROGER:

Please don't talk about that any more.

(*Off-stage, the sound of several machines. Mr. Roger is startled*)

ANNETTE:

What's the matter? Haven't you ever heard the sound of the machines before?

MR. ROGER:

They're putting them in the parks now.

ANNETTE:

So what? Is that any reason for you to leave off your Olympian calm? I don't see why.

MR. ROGER:

(*Standing up, painfully*)

Annie . . .

(*Leaning on his cane, trying to push Annette away*)

excuse me, but I want to get a little nearer. It's all I have left.

(*He moves off, stage left*)

ANNETTE:

(*Shouting*)

It's not enough for you to talk about them . . . you want to see them close up, admire how the flippers work? Working them yourself, of course, that's tiring, but if other people do it for you . . . you can always watch, can't you? And even from time to time

(*Sobbing*)

catch the three little girls falling into papa's trap!

(*By the time Annette is through speaking, Mr. Roger has already disappeared and Victor has been standing at stage right for some seconds. He is now behind Annette, who is sobbing. The sound of the machines can still be heard.*)

VICTOR:

(*Over Annette's shoulder*)
Good shot, Annette!

(*Annette gives a start and turns around*)

(*He laughs*)
That's what you call scoring a point: you've knocked him out, our pretty boy!
(*Noticing that Annette is crying*)
What's the matter, dear? Is what happened to the three cuties as bad as all that?
(*Pause*)
Well, for once Arthur wasn't romanticizing.

ANNETTE:

I advise you not to mention Arthur. Did he send you?

VICTOR:

Of course not.
(*Pause*)
Something new has happened, my dear. Arthur and I are through. We don't see each other any more. I'm not interested in ruining my career and associating with people like that. . . . Besides, anyone who sees Arthur has to see Sutter now. Last Saturday they were both at my house, during one of my consultations. Quarrels, shouts, blows, people getting hurt. You can't imagine what a scene it was.

And one episode like that could cost me my whole practice. And who had to bandage Mr. Arthur's head afterward? Victor, of course.

ANNETTE:

(*With an unhappy laugh*)

I know. The Corporation orphans are always fighting
among themselves.

VICTOR:

Listen, Annette. If you want to be friends with me, don't
talk about the Corporation any more either. Besides, it's
ancient history. You know it won't be long before nation-
alization, which by the way will be better for everyone
anyway, at least for you and me.

(*Pause*)

We've lost too much blood in this business already, my
dear. But there's no harm done if we each have a job;
now that I'm a doctor and you're a manicurist . . .

ANNETTE:

(*Laughing*)

Yes, we're just made to understand each other.

VICTOR:

Well, do you really want to be a manicurist?

ANNETTE:

(*Laughing*)

Perhaps you have something better in mind?

VICTOR:

Maybe.

(*Pause*)

Something right up your alley.

(*Annette laughs*)

Would you like to be my assistant?

(*Annette laughs harder. Victor tries to laugh, too, without understanding*)

Only, I warn you, you won't be twiddling your thumbs. I have a big practice now.
(*Still laughing*)
And thanks to what? Thanks to the pinball arcades. That's exactly the kind of place a doctor makes connections. All you have to do is gossip a little bit, make people have confidence in you . . .
(*He vaguely realizes that Annette's laughter is strange, hysterical. He is disconcerted for a moment, but continues.*)
Not to mention the fact that the arcades are a good place to play. You can choose your own machine and start in right away without asking any favors, and above all, it's better than
(*Laughing*)
carrying on a conversation with Mrs. Duranty.

(*Annette goes on laughing*)

SCENE ELEVEN

(*At Mrs. Duranty's. At stage center, slightly to the left, lying on two chairs, Annette's body, her long hair hanging down. Upstage a table and several other chairs. Mrs. Duranty is standing in front of the corpse, holding its head in her hands. Victor is sitting stage right, his head down.*)

MRS. DURANTY:
In front of the pinball arcade! I had to find her . . . like this, right in front of the pinball arcade . . .
(*Shouting*)
I always said those places were a terrible thing, nothing good will ever come of them. Dorothy, my little Dorothy . . . for me you're still Dorothy. That's what your mother called you, and Charles too.
(*She crosses herself*)
And when I think of that Arthur, all by himself . . . Oh, of course, it's his fault, but that's the way he is, Arthur . . . he talks and talks while Sutter, brute though he is . . . Poor Arthur! All alone, all swollen like that, with his big bandage around his head . . .
(*Pause*)

You ought to go see him all the same, Mr. Victor. He's so fond of you, you know. He asks for you every day. I don't know what to say any more. I suppose he hasn't been very nice to you, but look, he wasn't very nice to her either.
(*Pointing to Annette*)
And yet, at the end she talked about him all the time . . . not Mr. Roger. Why even last night, right here . . .
(*She cries*)
Poor little Annie. Those last days weren't happy for you, but what could you do about it? At your age, you shouldn't live alone.

VICTOR:
(*Raising his head*)
Don't babble on like that. I can tell you didn't see Annette yesterday. If you'd seen her you'd know that she hasn't been living alone the last three weeks.
(*He stands up and shouts*)
She's been living with me!

MRS. DURANTY:
With you? No, Mr. Victor, she didn't tell me that. I would have remembered that, you know.
(*With a senile laugh*)
A real lady . . . she kept her secrets to herself.

VICTOR:
Well then, why did you come to get me?
(*Beating his breast*)
Why me?

MRS. DURANTY:

Because . . . because you're a doctor.

(*Victor shrugs his shoulders and walks up and down*)

Don't be angry, Mr. Victor. You know how it is. When something terrible happens, you get a doctor . . . and since you've always taken care of me so nicely . . .

(*In a low voice, confidentially*)

And then, that's not all. We'll have to clear up this business ourselves . . . the police won't do anything. I know what they're like. . . . They're all paid by Algerians.

(*To the body*)

Don't worry, Annie. Mrs. Duranty will avenge you.

(*Turing toward Victor*)

So I thought, Mr. Victor, that maybe you'd know something.

(*Suddenly snarling*)

Since *you* go to the pinball arcades . . .

VICTOR:

(*Transfixed*)

The pinball arcades . . . always criticizing the pinball arcades—she, you, everybody. Why shouldn't I go to them? Why should I go into mourning for the Corporation? Was I ever married to the Corporation? Did anyone ever make a fuss over me there? Was I ever allowed to speak?

(*Pause*)

There's only one person in the world who wants me: Arthur. And why? So I can take off his bandage for him. But I don't have any bandage. All I have is my own head.

MRS. DURANTY:

Now, now, Mr. Victor. Looks don't count for a man . . . and they don't matter much for us either. We're pretty when someone loves us . . .

(*Laughing*)

If you had only seen me once . . . I didn't have my arthritis then . . . I was lively . . . I used to prance . . .

(*Victor sits down again stage right*)

Oooh! I shouldn't even mention words like that.

(*She sits down painfully, holding her kidneys*)

Mr. Victor, it's funny, you know. I did everything you told me. I took that prescription but . . .

(*Enter Sutter stage left, almost in rags. He has difficulty remaining standing, and he uses his arms the way a tight-rope walker uses a pole. He is more compulsive than ever, but this time the machine is turning in the void*)

SUTTER:

So no one says hello to Sutter any more? Just because he appears at the fatal hour of midnight? Hmmm? I happened to be going by, and noticing that your windows were lit . . .

(*Pause*)

Good God, you look as if you were at a funeral.

MRS. DURANTY:

That's the word for it, Mr. Sutter.

(*Pointing to Annette's body which Sutter has not even noticed*)

Look what's happened to us.

SUTTER:

  (*Approaching the body*)

  Why, it's Annette! Is she dead?

  (*Pause*)

  It must have been an accident. Poor Annie! I knew it would happen. She always crossed the streets without looking, like a madwoman! I always tried to warn her. . . . Yes, we made it up between us and we saw each other from time to time.

VICTOR:

  (*Half to himself*)

  I never thought she would.

SUTTER:

  So you still think Sutter was a renegade. Well, I was playing a double game, old friend. Annette could have told you if she had wanted to, if she had wanted to tell her secrets to her *old* boyfriend's *old* friend.

(*During Sutter's speech, Victor takes his coat and exits without a word. No one notices he is gone*)

MRS. DURANTY:

  But, Mr. Sutter, that had changed too. It wasn't Arthur any more, it was Mr. Victor.

  (*She turns around as if to take Victor as her witness and discovers his absence; she throws up her hands*)

  Oh!

SUTTER:

  (*Who still hasn't noticed anything*)

  Devilish little girl!

(*Sutter staggers, leans on the table, and finally sits down on a chair with his feet stretched out on another one*)
Forgive me, Mrs. Duranty, but I feel a little tired suddenly . . . overwork . . . it's only natural.
(*Pause*)
Besides, because of all this work I haven't had a moment all day . . . to restore my strength. . . . You wouldn't happen to have a snack . . . a sandwich . . . anything?

MRS. DURANTY:
I . . . I haven't much, Mr. Sutter, but maybe if I look hard I can find . . .

(*Still holding her kidneys, she goes to look for some bread and cheese, which she brings to Sutter. A long silence while Sutter greedily eats his sandwich. Mrs. Duranty, who has timidly taken refuge in a chair stage right, gradually dozes, her mouth open, while Sutter speaks*)

SUTTER:
(*Who seems to have recovered his strength because of the sandwich, turning toward the corpse*)
Poor kid. But it's ridiculous! The chips are never down for good. Not for anyone.
(*Standing up*)
As long as you live, you're on the go, and the wheel keeps turning and as long as it does . . .
(*He bursts out laughing, then turning toward Mrs. Duranty, who is now snoring*)
I could have let myself go too . . . but at the last moment I got the picture . . . and I decided to take a change of air

for good. Yes, the sleeping traveler inside me awakened and called and I answered, "Here!" Import-export, U.S.A. How does that sound to you? As for working here, it's a waste of time, a lot of noise for nothing. As for the machines people around here think up . . . I'm sorry for the players.

(*Walking back and forth across the stage like a madman, while Mrs. Duranty snores louder and louder*)

In the States, they have big ideas. They see things on a big scale. Ideas have consequences, people take action, the bidding rises, people put money on you, double or nothing, the winner and still champ, drive, it's all drive. Once you've got drive, the machine runs itself and it runs and runs . . .

(*Sutter walks so heavily and so fast that he knocks Annette's body off the chairs as he passes. Mrs. Duranty is still snoring.*)

SCENE TWELVE

(*At Victor's. A ping-pong table with one peculiar character-istic: it is oddly divided into eight black and white squares. The net, however, is quite orthodox. Arthur and Victor, now seventy, with white hair and holding paddles, are about to play a game. Victor is dressed as a very correct old gentle-man. He is wearing glasses. Arthur, who has taken off his coat, is wearing a dirty, torn shirt. At the rear is a scoreboard on which are written in chalk the points won respectively by the two players: A-2, V-3.*)

VICTOR:
  (*Raising his paddle*)
  Play?

ARTHUR:
  (*Raising his*)
  Ready!

(*Victor serves, Arthur misses the shot. The ball falls off the table*)

VICTOR:
  (*Laughing*)
  Aced!

ARTHUR:

Listen, Victor, you know we finally agreed, after a number of consultations, to divide the sides into squares. And now you accuse me of missing your serve when you yourself missed because you obviously served in the wrong square.

VICTOR:

Arthur, you know as well as I do that I served it on the right side.

ARTHUR:

I tell you, you served it in the wrong *square* and now you say it was on the right side. So either you're willfully and consciously confusing the squares with the sides, which would prove, or at least would seem to prove . . .

VICTOR:

Listen, Arthur, I consider that a ball not returned is a shot missed. Now you didn't return it, so it's you who missed it. In other words, you're talking about the squares and sides so you won't have to go look for it. Because you know perfectly well that the person who misses the ball has to go look for it.

ARTHUR:

On condition that the error was made not by the server but the receiver, or at least by the player who was supposed to receive it.

VICTOR:

(*Stamps his foot*)
All right, I'll look for it.
(*He stoops over and looks for the ball*)

It's not here.
(*Straightening up*)
I don't know where it is, but it's not here.
(*He goes to the blackboard*)

ARTHUR:

What are you doing?

VICTOR:

(*Giving himself a point*)
You can see. I'm giving myself a point.

ARTHUR:

(*Letting his hands fall to his sides and hanging his head*)
Then you absolutely refuse to play according to the division into squares and sides? Of course, it's perfectly possible that this division might not be absolutely necessary
. . . but if you feel it's not only unnecessary but even that it should be rejected, I don't see why you accepted it, or pretended to accept it . . .

VICTOR:

(*Brandishing his paddle*)
You're not going to start again like last Sunday.

ARTHUR:

Last Sunday?

VICTOR:

Exactly. Last Sunday. I suppose we didn't play last Sunday? And I suppose you didn't have your indigestion last Sunday?

ARTHUR:

Yes, I had indigestion, but not because I had eaten too many croquettes the way you thought. I had indigestion because I usually don't eat enough during the week and especially because I never eat croquettes. The trouble is that you don't ask yourself what I eat during the week.

VICTOR:

No, I don't ask myself because I know what it is. And I also know that you'd eat more if you'd taken a little more interest . . .

ARTHUR:

Yes, I don't make as much as you do at Universal Correspondence, but then, I don't have to work as hard as you do at Universal Correspondence.

VICTOR:

There's no use shifting the problem. You know perfectly well that if I mentioned your indigestion it was only because just before having that indigestion you made such a scene.

ARTHUR:

I made a scene?

VICTOR:

Yes, and a rather painful scene at that. At least I consider it painful when you're playing in a person's house to criticize that person for having so few balls.

ARTHUR:

I wasn't criticizing you for having so few balls. I merely

told you, and I'm still telling you, that it's almost impossible to play with less than five balls, and all things considered I wasn't entirely wrong, since we're always—and now in particular—looking for a ball for one reason or another.

VICTOR:

Listen, Arthur, I know how much a ball costs and I also know how much a patient brings in. Not much.

ARTHUR:

(*Who for the last moment has been looking for the ball in order not to listen to Victor, straightening up*)
It's really unbearable how these balls don't want to stay on the table and keep rolling off in all directions.

VICTOR:

They roll off in *one* direction, which is the direction they've been served in. Now since I served it, the ball has to be on your side.

ARTHUR:

I don't see why it has to be on my side. It might just as well have rolled onto your side afterward, and that's why you should be looking around on your side.
(*He then gets down on all fours and continues looking. Victor does the same*)
Anyway, I can't see anything over here, that's for sure.

VICTOR:

(*On all fours*)
You might see something and the ball in particular if you wore glasses like everyone else.

ARTHUR:

(*Still on all fours*)

Well, *you* wear glasses and . . .

VICTOR:

(*Who has just found the ball, standing up, triumphantly*)

Yes, I wear glasses and I've got the ball too! Play?

ARTHUR:

(*Running to his place*)

Ready!

(*Victor serves the ball, Arthur returns it, Victor misses, Arthur laughs*)

You missed! Four all. Mark it down.

VICTOR:

Don't just say the first thing that comes into your head. The score was 4-2, so now it's 4-3. At best.

ARTHUR:

No, not at best. At best, I'd have five and you four. And since just now . . .

(*Victor shrugs his shoulders but nevertheless marks Arthur's score*)

VICTOR:

(*Who this time has found the ball without difficulty*)

Play?

ARTHUR:

Just a minute. After all, you could take a second to think every once in a while, a second to discuss. . . . It's the least we can do, I should think, since we're alone and quiet and don't have to hurry and we . . .

VICTOR:

(*Impatient*)

Play?

(*Without waiting for an answer, he furiously serves and of course Arthur doesn't return the ball*)

ARTHUR:

(*Throwing away his paddle*)

Oh no, oh no. That's a real Sutter play.

(*He sits on the table and crosses his arms in protest*)

VICTOR:

(*Throwing his paddle down too and also sitting on the table*)

It's your own fault. You should have been ready. And besides we have to settle once and for all what we're playing. *I'm* playing ping-pong!

ARTHUR:

(*Standing up*)

Ah, the squares bother you, do they? You want to go back to tennis; go on, admit it.

VICTOR:

(*Standing up*)

I've already explained a hundred times that in tennis there are sides, not squares. Now *I* want to get rid of not only the squares, but the sides, too. When will you understand that it's English that's mixing you up.

(*Furiously*)

"Table tennis," "table tennis!"

ARTHUR:

All I understand is that you want to play pure and simple, without squares or sides . . .

(*Almost shouting*)

All right, I don't care. Let's try it.

VICTOR:

No, we're not going to try it until you admit . . .

ARTHUR:

(*Grabbing his paddle*)

All right. I admit it, I admit it. Play?

VICTOR:

(*Who has rushed to pick up his*)

Ready!

(*Arthur serves, Victor returns but into the net. Victor stamps his foot*)

Damn!

ARTHUR:

You see, you missed anyway.

VICTOR:

I beg your pardon, I didn't miss. It's the net that stopped the ball.

ARTHUR:

(*Exasperated*)

Oh, so it's the net that bothers you, is it? Well, nothing's forcing us to play with a net. Before tennis was invented, they played without a net. All right, you want me to take away the net?

VICTOR:

I never said you should take away the net. It's you who mentioned taking away the net.

(*Provocatively*)

If you want to take away the net . . .

ARTHUR:

(*Almost laughing*)

Sure I want to take away the net.

(*He removes the net with Victor's help*)

Play?

VICTOR:

Ready!

(*They exchange two or three volleys*)

VICTOR:

(*Whose paddle slips out of his hands*)

Arthur . . .

ARTHUR:

What's the matter?

VICTOR:

(*Picking up the ball*)

It . . . it slipped out of my hands.

ARTHUR:

Your paddle?

VICTOR:

Of course my paddle. What do you think slipped out of my hands?

ARTHUR:

(Bursting into "Homeric" laughter)
Great! That's just great! You want to play without a
paddle now? You don't think you have to have a paddle
just because you have a ball? Well, maybe you're right.
All right then, go on. Serve. Yes, with your hand. What
are you waiting for?
(He throws his paddle away)

VICTOR:

(Laughing with Arthur)
I dare you!

*(Victor serves the ball with his hand. Arthur catches it and
throws it back. There are several volleys growing wilder and
wilder; sometimes the ball bounces on the table, sometimes
on the floor. In order to catch it, the two old men make tremendous, spectacular, flabby leaps. Arthur is still laughing,
Victor too, although he is growing noticeably winded. His
gestures are becoming slower and weaker than Arthur's.)*

VICTOR:

(Panting, but still playing)
Well, you know, the truth . . .

*(Arthur has thrown the ball particularly high. Victor leaps
for it but—his heart?—falls heavily to the floor.)*

ARTHUR:

(Panic-stricken)
Victor! Victor!

Curtain